Ready for
IELTS

2nd Edition

Workbook
without Answers

Louis Rogers

macmillan
education

+ Audio CDs

Macmillan Education Limited
4 Crinan Street
London N1 9XW
Companies and representatives throughout the world

ISBN 978-1-786-32865-6 (with Answers)
ISBN 978-1-786-32866-3 (without Answers)

Designed by xen
Illustrated by xen pp. 44, 47, 50, 79, 88
Cover design by Macmillan Education Limited
Cover photograph by Getty Images/Ascent/PKS Media Inc
Picture research by Julie-anne Wilce

Author's acknowledgements
Louis Rogers would like to say thank you to the team at Macmillan for their expertise and patience.

The publishers would like to thank Sam McCarter.

The author and publishers would like to thank the following for permission to reproduce their photographs: **Alamy** Mathias Beinling p63, epa european pressphoto agency b.v. p100, Oliver Furrer p23, MITO images p76, Niday Picture Library pp17, 61, NPC Collection p62, Matthias Riedinger p78, State Archives of Florida p29, Feng Yu p108; **Getty Images** Baranozdemir p102, Levi Bianco p105, Walter Bibikow p70, Alex Brylov p40, Classic Stock/H. Armstrong Roberts p113, Dutch Scenery p13, EyeEm/Danil Rudenko p51, Mike Harrington p110, Horsche p31, JGI/Jamie Grill p53, Jose Luis Pelaez Inc p56, Jupiterimages p21, Konstik p95, Maremagnum p64, Maya p82, Mikkelwilliam p14, Minden Pictures/Hedgehog House/Colin Monteath p33, Aleksandar Nakic p39, Alexander Nikiforov p93, Judd Patterson p107, People Images p85, Pixelfit p7, pius99 p68(B), Ariel Skelley p115, Streluk p68(C), Klaus Vedfelt p58, iara venanzi p45, vgajic p4, Volanthevist p69(E), Wandersmann p38, Dong Wenjie p103; **Shutterstock** BBA Photography p75, f11photo p68(A), JetKat p98, Thomas La Mela p28, Mipan p36, Multitel p69(D), Pkchai p9.

The author and publishers are grateful for permission to reprint the following copyright material:
pp7–8 Extract from 'How to choose your inner circle: With friends like these …' by Katy Guest, copyright © The Independent 2016. First published in *The Independent* 01.07.16. Reprinted by permission of the publisher; p11 Data from the graph 'Snapchat rising in popularity with youth'. Source: Edison Research/ Triton Digital – The Infinite Dial 2015 http://www.edisonresearch.com/the-infinite-dial-2015/, copyright © 2016 Edison Research. All rights reserved. Reprinted by permission of Edison Research; p16 Extract from 'Oxford Big Ideas Geography History 9' by Mark Easton, Geraldine Carrodus, Tim Delaney, Kate McArthur & Richard Smith, copyright © Oxford University Press, www.oup.com.au. Reproduced by permission of Oxford University Press Australia; pp23–24 Extract from 'What Motivates Extreme Athletes to Take Huge Risks?' by Melissa Dahl, copyright © 2016 New York Media LLC. Reprinted by permission of the publisher; p26 Data from 'The Millenials', copyright © 2016 National Sporting Goods Association. Data published on Sports Business Research Network http://sbrnet.com/Blog/July-2015/The-Millennials.aspx. Reprinted by permission of National Sporting Goods Association; pp31–32 Adapted material from the article 'The Luck Factor' by Richard Wiseman, copyright © Richard Wiseman 2003. Published in the Skeptical Inquirer May/June 2003 by The Committee for the Scientific Investigation of Claims of the Paranormal. Reprinted by permission of the author; p39–40 Extract from 'Beyond botox – the future of anti-ageing' by Anna Magee, copyright © Telegraph Media Group Limited 2016. First published in *The Daily Telegraph* 30.05.16. Reprinted by permission of the publisher; p40 Extract from 'World's first anti-ageing drug could see humans live to 120' by Sarah Knapton, copyright © Telegraph Media Group Limited 2015. First published in *The Daily Telegraph* 29.11.15. Reprinted by permission of the publisher; p42 Data from 'Consumers in 2030: Forecasts and projections for life in 2030', copyright © Which? 2013. Reprinted by permission of Which?; p45 Extract from 'A Brief History of Chocolate' by Amanda Fiegl, copyright © 2008 Smithsonian Institution. Reprinted with permission from Smithsonian Enterprises. All rights reserved. Reproduction in any medium is strictly prohibited without permission from Smithsonian Institution; p45 Extracts from 'How Chocolate is Made from Cacao', published on www.lakechamplainchocolates.com, copyright © 2013 Lake Champlain Chocolates. All Rights Reserved. Reprinted by permission of the publisher; p53 Extract from 'Staff should start work at 10am to avoid 'torture' of sleep deprivation' by Sarah Knapton, copyright © Telegraph Media Group Limited 2015. First published in *The Daily Telegraph* 08.09.15. Reprinted by permission of the publisher; p53 Extract from 'Sleep deprivation 'as bad as smoking'' by Laura Donnelly, copyright © Telegraph Media Group Limited 2015. First published in *The Daily Telegraph* 27.07.15. Reprinted by permission of the publisher; p53 Extract from 'Study proves what we already knew: being sleep deprived does the same to your brain as being drunk' by Sonia Haria, copyright © Telegraph Media Group Limited 2016. First published in *The Daily Telegraph* 07.04.16. Reprinted by permission of the publisher; p61 Extract from '12 Maps That Changed the World' by Uri Friedman, copyright © 2013 The Atlantic Media Co., as first published in theatlantic.com. All rights reserved. Distributed by Tribune Content Agency. Reprinted by permission of Tribune Content Agency; p70 Extract from 'Benefits of Historic Preservation', published by the Washington Trust for Historic Preservation on www.preservewa.org, copyright © 2016. All rights reserved. Reprinted by permission of the publisher; p71 Extracts from 'The art of regeneration: Urban renewal through cultural activity' by Charles Landry, Lesley Greene, François Matarasso & Franco Bianchini, copyright © 1996 Charles Landry, Lesley Greene, François Matarasso and Franco Bianchini. First published 1996 by Comedia, The Round, Bournes Green, Stroud, Gloucestershire, GL6 7NL. Reprinted by permission of Charles Landry; pp78–79 Extract from 'The Floating Piers' by Christo and Jeanne-Claude, copyright © 2017 Christo; pp85–86 Extract from 'The Return of the Multi-Generational Family Household', Pew Research Center, Washington DC (March 2010) http://www.pewsocialtrends.org/2010/03/18/the-return-of-the-multi-generational-family-household/. Reprinted by permission of Pew Research Center; pp85–86 Statistics taken from graphs in the article 'In Post-Recession Era, Young Adults Drive Continuing Rise in Multi-Generational Living' by Richard Fry and Jeffrey S. Passel, copyright © 2017 Pew Research Center; pp95–96 Extracts from 'Geological History' and 'Species Arrival to Galapagos', published on www.galapagos.org, copyright © 2016 Galapagos Conservancy. Reprinted by permission of the publisher; p103 Extract from 'The rise of the mega-city will change the global economy forever' by Allister Heath, copyright © Telegraph Media Group Limited 2014. First published in *The Daily Telegraph* 28.08.14. Reprinted by permission of the publisher; p106 Data from 'UK Energy In Brief 2015', Department of Energy & Climate Change, copyright © Crown copyright 2015. Contains public sector information licensed under the Open Government Licence v3.0; pp109, 124 Adapted material from 'Happiness: Lessons from a New Science' by Richard Layard, copyright © Richard Layard 2005. Reprinted by permission of Penguin Books UK & United Agents; pp110–111 Extract from 'What's the secret to happiness? Scientists may have found the answer' by Mark Molloy, copyright © Telegraph Media Group Limited 2016. First published in *The Daily Telegraph* 23.05.16. Reprinted by permission of the publisher; pp110–111 Extract from 'Money CAN buy happiness – if you spend in the right way, according to 'groundbreaking Cambridge study' by James Connington, copyright © Telegraph Media Group Ltd. First published in *The Daily Telegraph* 07.04.16. Reprinted by permission of the publisher; pp110–111 Extract from 'The 33 things that will make you happy…and the seven that definitely won't' by Sarah Knapton, copyright © Telegraph Media Group Limited 2016. First published in *The Daily Telegraph* 03.02.16. Reprinted by permission of the publisher; pp110–111 Extract from 'Men's happiness in later life is determined by the age of 27' by Jonathan Wells, copyright © Telegraph Media Group Limited 2015. First published in *The Daily Telegraph* 18.09.15. Reprinted by permission of the publisher; pp110–111 Extract from 'Why leaving Facebook has made me happier' by Rachel Halliwell, copyright © Telegraph Media Group Limited 2015. First published in *The Daily Telegraph* 13.11.15. Reprinted by permission of the publisher; pp110–111 Extract from 'The secret to true happiness? Not being too happy. Here's how to be content instead' by Rebecca Reid, copyright © Telegraph Media Group Limited 2016. First published in *The Daily Telegraph* 04.03.16. Reprinted by permission of the publisher; p114 Data from the Working Paper 18992 for The National Bureau of Economic Research, 'Subjective Well-Being and Income: Is There any Evidence of Satiation?' by Betsey Stevenson & Justin Wolfers, copyright © 2013 by Betsey Stevenson and Justin Wolfers. All rights reserved; Sample IELTS Listening and Reading Answer Sheet. Reproduced with permission of Cambridge English Language Assessment © UCLES 2016.

Printed and bound in Poland by CGS

2021

Contents

1   We are all friends now   4

2   Technology – now and then   12

3   Thrill seekers   20

4   Global issues and opportunities   28

5   The future   36

6   The fruits of nature   44

7   The world of work and education   52

8   Mapping the world   60

9   What is beauty?   68

10   Is it art?   76

11   The family and society   84

12   Travelling around the world   92

13   The importance of infrastructure   100

14   Money and well-being   108

Listening scripts   116

Wordlist   125

1 We are all friends now

Vocabulary: Describing people

Wordlist on page 211 of the Student's Book.

1 Match the words **1–12** to the definitions **a–l**.

1 artistic		**a** keen to try new or exciting things
2 supportive		**b** a person who speaks a lot
3 adventurous		**c** does not easily get annoyed
4 talkative		**d** involving a lot of imagination and new ideas
5 sporty		**e** a person who enjoys doing physical things
6 patient		**f** thinking about the feelings and needs of other people
7 ambitious		**g** *being good at things such as painting, music, etc*
8 creative		**h** determined to be rich, successful, etc
9 considerate		**i** working hard and carefully to do things well
10 conscientious		**j** someone who is sympathetic and you can rely on
11 helpful		**k** someone you can trust
12 reliable		**l** a person who is happy to help others

2 Complete the sentences using an appropriate adjective from exercise 1.

1 My cousin is totally _____ . She always does what she says she will do.

2 He's already extremely successful, but he's so _____ he wants to achieve more.

3 Nick's really _____ . There's never a moment's silence.

4 My mother-in-law is very _____ . She has exhibited her work in a local gallery.

5 They are always _____ . They will go anywhere, do anything and eat anything!

6 Every week, she posts on Facebook about a race or competition she has taken part in. She's such a _____ person.

7 Thank you for being so _____ . It really helped me at a difficult time.

8 My sister is very _____ with young children. She never gets angry or cross.

9 My brother is so _____ . He doesn't just read stories to his children. He writes them as well.

10 I think I'm really _____ . I always try to think about other people first.

11 If you want to be _____ , you could take the dog for a walk.

12 They are very _____ . They always do their homework and check the answers before giving it to the teacher.

3 Complete the sentences with the adjective form of the words in brackets.

1 My sister is a very _____ person. She always thinks about other people. (care)

2 She's so _____ . She makes me laugh a lot. (humour)

3 They are a _____ team. I love watching them. (talent)

4 I love how _____ she is. She's the centre of attention at every party. (sociability)

5 My mother's very _____ . She always does well in quizzes. (knowledge)

6 He never gets nervous. He's a very _____ presenter. (confidence)

7 She'll do anything to help anyone. She's such a _____ person. (generosity)

8 They are really not very _____ . They are always late. (punctuality)

Listening
Section 1

🎧 **1.1 SECTION 1 *Questions 1–10***

Questions 1–6

Complete the notes below.

Write **NO MORE THAN TWO WORDS AND/OR A NUMBER** *for each answer.*

Summer holiday camps

> **Example:**
> Junior camp: ages 5–10
> Senior camp: ages ....11–16.....

Senior camp

1 From .... am to 6.00 pm (can also start at 7 am)

2 Monday, Wednesday and Friday mornings: .... activities

3 Tuesday and Thursday mornings: .... activities

4 Weekday afternoons: ....

5 Optional trip to .... : all day on first Wednesday

6 Family BBQ: every .... evening

Questions 7–10

Complete the notes below.

Write **NO MORE THAN ONE WORD AND/OR A NUMBER** *for each answer.*

Booking and costs

You must book a **7** .... in advance

Normal cost per child: **8** £............................... per week

9 .... per cent discount for each extra child

Personal details

Parent's name: Andrea

Parent's contact number: **10** ....

Language focus 1: Likes and dislikes

(G) Grammar reference on page 219 of the Student's Book.

1 Choose the correct verbs, **a–c**, that can be used to complete the sentences. There may be more than one possible answer for each sentence.

1 I _____ to study in the UK.

   a 'd like   **b** want   **c** dislike

2 She _____ studying Chemistry when she was at school.

   a loves   **b** enjoyed   **c** chose

3 My brother _____ to learn another foreign language.

   a 'd enjoy   **b** wants   **c** can't stand

4 They _____ to go to university in another country.

   a 'd love   **b** like   **c** wanted

5 She really _____ going shopping. She goes every weekend.

   a enjoys   **b** enjoying   **c** preferred

6 He is fond of _____ other countries. He has at least three holidays a year.

   a visit   **b** visiting   **c** visited

2 Complete the sentences with phrases from the box. There may be more than one possible answer for each sentence.

appeals to me	don't seem to take any pleasure in
get a lot of pleasure from	really likes to
want to	get enormous enjoyment from

1 When I retire I _____ live in the countryside not the city.

2 You rarely see young people walking in the countryside. They _____ it.

3 Joining a gym _____ , but I don't think I would go often enough.

4 She _____ run. She goes three or four times a week.

5 I _____ travelling. It helps me relax and unwind.

6 Many people _____ eating different foods and trying unusual restaurants while they are travelling.

3 Complete the sentences with *love/like/don't like/hate* + the correct form of the verbs in the box. Use the faces to help you.

KEY: ☺ = like; ☺☺ = love; ☹ = don't like; ☹☹ = hate

eat	go	meet	play	read	study	listen	work

1 He _____ for the bank. He wants to find a new job. ☹☹

2 They _____ Indian food. ☺

3 I _____ Chinese. I find the writing really difficult. ☹

4 She _____ on holiday to hot countries. ☺☺

5 I _____ my friends in the shopping mall. ☺

6 We _____ team sports, but we like going for a run. ☹☹

7 He _____ old books. He prefers reading modern novels. ☹

8 I _____ to the radio in the morning while eating breakfast. ☺☺

Reading
Questions 1–14

READING PASSAGE

*You should spend about 20 minutes on **Questions 1–14**, which are based on the Reading Passage below.*

Questions 1–7

The Reading Passage has eight paragraphs, **A–H**.

*Choose the correct heading for paragraphs **B–H** from the list of headings below.*

List of Headings

   i The personal impact of friendship

  ii The right amount and quality of friends

 iii Strong relationships with best friend

  iv What is friendship?

   v Communities aren't isolated

  vi Understanding ourselves

 vii Individual differences and the effect on community

viii The decline of friendship

  ix New studies on friendship

   x Changes in the selection process

Example:	Answer:
Paragraph **A**	iv

1 Paragraph **B**

2 Paragraph **C**

3 Paragraph **D**

4 Paragraph **E**

5 Paragraph **F**

6 Paragraph **G**

7 Paragraph **H**

What friends do we need?

A When Aristotle was asked, in the 4th century BC, what defines a friend, he had no doubts. A friend is 'one soul inhabiting two bodies,' he said, adding: 'Without friends no one would choose to live, though he had all other goods.' In this century, it is a little more complicated. A startling discovery in the *American Sociological Review* found 25 per cent of Americans do not have a single friend. That is, nobody 'with whom to discuss matters important to them,' said the researchers. The average number of friends was two. Yet modern demands on our time can take a deep toll on friendships.

B Two books aim to help us through the maze. *Vital Friends: The People You Can't Afford to Live Without* by Tom Rath, advises readers to evaluate the roles played by their friends, ensuring eight essential friendship types are represented. *Rethinking Friendship: Hidden Solidarities Today* by Liz Spencer and Ray Pahl looks at the different kinds of friendships in the internet age.

C Rath is a *New York Times* bestselling author, and leads research and consulting at Gallup. He analysed more than five million interviews to try to define what Plato said he never could: what is friendship? The result is *Vital Friends*, and it reaches startling conclusions. If you ask people why they became homeless, why their marriage failed or why they overeat, he says, they do not blame it on poverty or mobility; they blame it on a lack of friendships. If your best friend eats healthily, he discovered, you are five times more likely to have a healthy diet yourself. His interviewees rated friendship as being more than five times as important as physical intimacy in the success of a marriage. He also found patients with heart disease are twice as likely to die if they do not have three or four close social connections.

D Ray Pahl's *Rethinking Friendship* is based on in-depth interviews conducted over seven years. He finds the quality of our friendships has a huge influence on the amount of satisfaction we draw from life. 'Individuals with no real friends at work have only a one in 12 chance of feeling engaged in their job,' he says. But the quantity, as well as the quality of friends, does matter. Some people can have three or four close friends and be very happy, he believes. Others more extrovert prefer to have 10 or 15. But he is certain you need to have more than one friend to be satisfied in life. 'It is a very common mistake to expect one close friend to provide everything you need,' he says. 'And it can cause a lot of problems.'

E Dr Angela Carter, an occupational psychiatrist from Sheffield University, says: 'We are social animals. We need friends to hold a mirror up to us and show us what our behaviour looks like. They provide companionship and support, but the most important thing friends do is help us to work out who we are. Families cannot do that in the same way.' She has found people can struggle to find the friends that they need. 'We need to be quite strategic in our friendships. People think friends turn up from nowhere, and they grumble when they don't have any. You need to think, "What do I need from friends and am I being a good friend in return?" '

F In researching *Rethinking Friendship*, Pahl found little cause for the notion that society is becoming atomised and selfish. 'Friendship takes such a variety of different forms,' he says. 'I don't think people have fewer friends now. What is new is that in the past 50 years we have become more and more used to choosing friends, rather than accepting them as given.'

G Both authors did not find transient communities are all about networking and getting on. 'As people have learned to be consumers, maybe they have also learned to make choices among their friends,' says Pahl. 'But when people think about their close friends, those relationships are deep and trusting, not exploitative or self-seeking. People are probably loyal and decent, against what is cynically regarded as the current of the age.'

H So how many friends can one person reasonably support? 'I don't think it is useful or meaningful to put a number on it,' says Dr Carter. 'Psychologists use the term 'affiliation need', and society tells us we have a lot of it. In truth, some people need a lot of friends, others few.' 'It is fair to say, people with a more diverse and mixed group of friends have a more robust defence against the way the world works,' says Pahl. 'I don't want to be prescriptive, or the government will start saying that we need a Ministry of Mates. But if you can provide the circumstances for a more friendly society, then society will be happier and healthier.'

Questions 8–11

Complete the sentences below.

*Choose **NO MORE THAN TWO WORDS AND/OR A NUMBER** from the passage for each answer.*

8 A quarter of people from the USA are without a ....

9 People need .... different types of friend in their group.

10 People blame problems in their lives on not having enough ....

11 The .... of friendships and the number of friends is important.

Questions 12–14

Do the following statements agree with the information given in the Reading Passage?

Write:

> **TRUE** *if the statement agrees with the information*
>
> **FALSE** *if the statement contradicts the information*
>
> **NOT GIVEN** *if there is no information on this*

12 People don't find it easy to get the friendships they require.

13 Technology has changed friendship groups.

14 Everyone needs the same number of friends to be happy.

Language focus 2: Present simple, present continuous and past simple

(G) Grammar reference on page 219 of the Student's Book.

1 Transform the verb in brackets into the correct form of the present simple, present continuous or past simple.

An international student in Brazil

Where do you usually study?

I 1 _____ (study) at a university in London, but this month I 2 _____ (study) at São Paulo University in Brazil.

Why 3 _____ (choose) Brazil?

My university in England 4 _____ (have) an exchange programme with São Paulo University. I can 5 _____ (speak) some Portuguese and I 6 _____ (be) really interested in Brazilian culture.

Where 7 _____ (live) at the moment?

I 8 _____ (stay) with two Brazilian guys in a small flat.

What 9 _____ (do) in your free time?

I'm lucky, I 10 _____ (meet) lots of new people when I first got here. We often 11 _____ (go) to concerts, the cinema or the gym. It's similar to England, but here we usually 12 _____ (go) out much later at night.

What do you miss about home?

When I was in England, I 13 _____ (see) my family a lot more, but now I never 14 _____ (see) them. We often 15 _____ (chat) on social media, but it's not the same. They 16_____ (visit) me last month, which 17 _____ (be) great. Also, I absolutely 18 _____ (love) Brazilian food, but I want to eat a good curry!

2 Choose **a**, **b** or **c** to complete the sentences 1–8.

1 He _____ in the evening.

  a doesn't work   **b** not work   **c** isn't working

2 This month my cousin _____ with me.

  a lives   **b** is living   **c** lived

3 _____ to the gym last night?

  a Did you go   **b** Are you go   **c** You went

4 Did you go online this morning? _____

  a Yes, I do.   **b** Yes, I was.   **c** No, I didn't.

5 My friend Karl _____ watching football.

  a is hating   **b** hates   **c** hate

6 I _____ bake a cake for her birthday so I bought one.

  a couldn't   **b** wouldn't   **c** don't

7 Friendship _____ more important to me when I _____ young.

  a is   **b** was   **c** being

8 I _____ Management from 2012 to 2015.

  a study   **b** am studying   **c** studied

Writing
Task 1

1 Match the verbs of movement in the box to the correct image **1–9**.

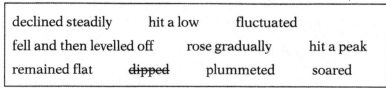

declined steadily	hit a low	fluctuated
fell and then levelled off	rose gradually	hit a peak
remained flat	~~dipped~~	plummeted	soared

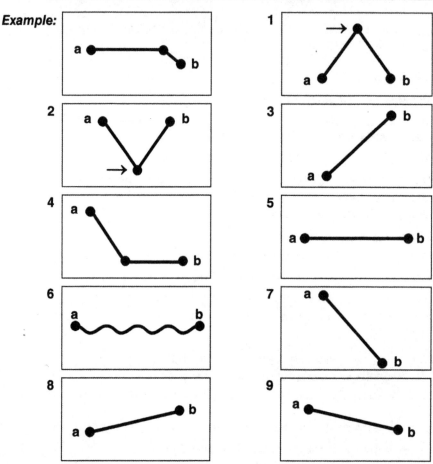

2 For sentences **1–6** below, <u>underline</u> the correct word in *italics*.

1 Levels of unemployment *declined/a decline* rapidly.

2 There was *a rise/rise* in levels of unemployment.

3 The year 2000 saw *a drop/drop* in high street purchases.

4 In 2015, household spending had *dip/a dip*.

5 The number of users *fell/a fall* by 15%.

6 Between 1970 and 1975 the numbers simply *fluctuated/a fluctuation*.

3 Rewrite sentences **1–3** below with nouns instead of verbs.

Example:

The proportion of students using social media dropped dramatically in January.
There was a dramatic drop in the proportion of students using social media in January.

1 The sales of mobile phones fluctuated in the first few months of last year.

2 The number of people studying engineering gradually declined until 2010.

3 Household income has risen steadily since 2010.

4 Look at the following Task 1 question and then answer questions **1–3** below.

WRITING TASK 1

You should spend about 20 minutes on this task.

> *The bar chart below shows social media use in Americans aged 12–24 between 2014 and 2015.*
>
> *Summarise the information by selecting and reporting the main features, and make comparisons where relevant.*

Write at least 150 words.

Social Media Usage Among American Youth (12–24)

Platform	2015	2014
Facebook	74%	80%
Instagram	59%	53%
Snapchat	57%	46%
Twitter	32%	36%
Vine	30%	30%
Tumblr	15%	22%

---

1 What does the bar chart show?

2 How long should you spend on the task?

3 What's the minimum you should write?

5 Complete the model answer using the correct form of the words in the box.

---

remain flat   decline (x2)   dip   soar   rise (x2)   plummet   change

---

The bar chart shows changes in social media use for 12–24-year-old Americans between 2014 and 2015. Three of the social media platforms **1** _____ in terms of their usage while two of the sites **2** _____ . The biggest **3** _____ is in the number of people using Tumblr, which **4** _____ from 22% of 12–24 years olds to just 15%. While Facebook **5** _____ by a similar amount, it still holds the position of the most popular social media site. The final site to show a fall in number of users from this demographic was Twitter. Here the fall was less dramatic, with the percentage **6** _____ by just 4%.

In contrast the number of users on Instagram and Snapchat **7** _____ during this time period. While Instagram went up steadily from 53% to 59%, Snapchat **8** _____ by 11% from 46% to 57%, nearly overtaking Instagram as the second most popular social media site. The final site shown in the bar chart, Vine, **9** _____ during this time period.

In conclusion, social media usage is incredibly popular with 12–24-year-old Americans. However, the popularity of each site is generally changing.

6 Look again at the model answer and answer questions **a–c** below.

  a Which sentence summarises the data?

  b Which change in social media use was the biggest?

  c Which change was the smallest?

Vocabulary: Verbs of cause and effect

Wordlist on page 211 of the Student's Book.

1 Rearrange the letters to make verbs of cause and effect. Then use the noun form of each verb to complete the crossword.

Down

1 aveandc _ _ _ _ _ _ _ _

2 magaed _ _ _ _ _ _ _

3 amrh _ _ _ _ _

4 tooperm _ _ _ _ _ _ _ _

5 radetteoier _ _ _ _ _ _ _ _ _ _ _

Across

6 pimevor _ _ _ _ _ _ _ _

7 fatecf _ _ _ _ _ _

8 niur _ _ _ _

9 uproced _ _ _ _ _ _ _ _

10 lutser _ _ _ _ _ _

11 caneneh _ _ _ _ _ _ _ _

12 yedrost _ _ _ _ _ _ _

2 Underline the verb/noun that describes change. Do these sentences talk about positive, negative or neutral changes?

1 It is debatable whether most scientific advances have been an enhancement to life or not.

2 The education department are keen to promote online learning. It's key to encouraging the right skills for life.

3 One result of population growth is increased harm to the environment.

4 What have been the effects of testing on education?

5 Some developments, such as the use of fossil fuels, have definitely damaged the environment.

6 China and Germany produce more technological products than any other country.

1.2 SECTION 2 Questions 11–20

Questions 11–15

Choose the correct letter, A, B or C.

House of tomorrow Exhibition

11 The exhibition of the House of tomorrow is being opened with

    A the Homes of the past show.

    B the Cities of the future exhibition.

    C the Technology of the modern world exhibition.

12 The exhibition is being funded by

    A the Technology and towns project.

    B research funding.

    C hi-tech companies.

13 Researchers found that the energy use of smart homes

    A means they usually make more than they consume.

    B is three times lower than traditional homes.

    C produces less energy than it uses.

14 In California, the state wants to reduce water usage

    A by thirty per cent.

    B by building more smart homes.

    C by twenty-five per cent.

15 The homes in the exhibition are made from

    A natural materials.

    B recycled plastics.

    C local materials.

Questions 16–20

Which criticism matches the original feature that has now been improved in smart homes?

*Choose **FIVE** answers from the box and write the correct letter, **A–F**, next to Questions 16–20.*

Original feature	
16 recipe books	....
17 ovens	....
18 bathroom scales	....
19 computer screens	....
20 lighting	....

Criticism
A did not give you enough detail
B too large and dirty
C bad for your health
D not precise timing
E inefficient and slow
F too dramatic and bright

Word building: Evaluating adjectives

1 For the adjectives **1–14** below, create synonyms using the words in the box.

in-	im-	un-	-less

Example:

1 <u>im</u>practical__   2 __significant__

3 __appealing__   4 __appropriate__

5 __acceptable__   6 __effective__

7 __perfect__   8 __hope__

9 __use__   10 __important__

11 __necessary__   12 __inspiring__

13 __convenient__   14 __valuable__

2 Complete the sentences with the words in brackets. Use a prefix or suffix when needed.

1 The answer is _____ . It's not possible to make it work. (practical)

2 It was the _____ solution. It worked exactly how we wanted it to. (perfect)

3 The idea is _____ to many governments because ultimately it saves the country money. (appealing)

4 Many people find the committee members _____ and want to replace them. (effective)

5 The situation is _____ . I don't think any of those solutions would work. (hope)

6 Technology quickly becomes _____ and obsolete. (use)

7 This kind of behaviour is _____ in my country. You would offend a lot of people. (acceptable)

8 It was one of the most _____ technological developments of the last century. It had such a major impact on our society. (significant)

9 The internet was one of the most _____ developments of the last century. It changed so many aspects of how we work and live. (important)

10 Not all technological developments are _____ . (necessary)

11 A good product with an _____ design can easily fail to become a success. (inspiring)

12 The internet has made _____ tasks, such as banking, much easier. (convenient)

13 Many technological developments, such as the invention of cars and planes, and the introduction of factories, have been _____ to the environment. (harm)

14 Using social media at work is _____ . It should be kept to your private life. (appropriate)

3 For sentences **1–8** below, <u>underline</u> the correct word in *italics*.

1 Many people feel it is a valuable idea and *worthless/worthwhile* pursuing.

2 The idea could be an *ineffective/effective* solution as it solves a number of underlying issues.

3 The chemicals are harmful to people and are therefore *safe/unsafe* to use.

4 The cost of developing better safety procedures would be cheap and certainly *significant/insignificant* financially for a company as rich as this one.

5 Some people think that qualifications are *useful/useless* without work experience.

6 One of the most *valuable/valueless* suggestions was to reorganise the structure of the company to be more efficient.

7 The idea appeared *harmful/harmless* enough but in fact the consequences of it were irreversible.

8 It was *appropriate/inappropriate* for the other competitors to talk to the different teams because of the risk of cheating.

Language focus 1: Past simple and present perfect

G Grammar reference on page 220 of the Student's Book.

1 Put the verbs in brackets in the correct form of the present perfect or past simple.

1 The economy in Britain _____ since the Industrial Revolution. (decline)

2 China _____ to be one of the main economies in the world. (rise)

3 The World Fair _____ an event for countries to show their skills and talent to the world. (be)

4 IBM _____ some of the first home computers. (make)

5 When we _____ young, we _____ technology at school at all. (be/use)

6 I first _____ to America in 2005. I _____ there three times since. (go/be)

7 I _____ French at school, but I _____ it once in the last 10 years. (study/speak)

8 I _____ my first job as a lawyer in 2010. I _____ in the sector ever since. (get/work)

2 Put the verb in brackets into the correct form of the past simple active or passive.

1 Iron _____ in more and more buildings. (use)

2 Britain _____ the Industrial Revolution. (lead)

3 Conditions _____ poor for many people during the Industrial Revolution. (be)

4 Steam engines _____ energy. (generate)

5 Cotton _____ in hotter climates. (grow)

6 People _____ from rural areas to urban ones. (move)

7 Clothes _____ by machines. (produce)

8 The economy _____ by small business owners. (dominate)

3 Rewrite the sentences in exercise 2 to make active sentences passive and passive sentences active where it is logical.

Reading
Questions 1–13

READING PASSAGE

*You should spend about 20 minutes on **Questions 1–13**, which are based on the Reading Passage below.*

Some of the most important developments and innovations of the Industrial Revolution took place in the production of cotton, wool, coal and iron. However, arguably the most important 'invention' of the Industrial Revolution was not a single item of equipment or technology at all. Instead, it was a way of producing goods on a large scale using many workers and specialised machinery on one site. This method of production became known as the factory system.

Before the introduction of the factory system, manufacturing often took place in small workshops or in local workers' cottages (hence the term 'cottage industries'). Local traders and crafts people such as blacksmiths, wheelwrights (wheel makers), cartwrights (cart makers), potters, millers and weavers used their skills, strength or water power to largely hand-make items. In contrast, the factory system brought together large numbers of workers in a single site or factory. Few of these workers were skilled because most of the manufacturing was done by machines. Instead, the many factory workers performed tasks that were repetitive and required little skill. Many of the machines used for processes like spinning, weaving and paper manufacturing were powered at first by water using waterwheels, then by steam and finally by electricity. The factory system itself was made possible through a combination of the technological innovations and knowledge that emerged during this period.

Crompton's mule was invented in 1779 by Samuel Crompton by combining the spinning jenny's carriage and the water frame's rollers. It allowed a single power source to spin multiple machines, and worked with wool or cotton yarns. However, it still required a skilled weaver to operate. These spinning mules were developed further so they could be operated by unskilled workers. Steam power was later applied to the spinning mules for use in cotton-spinning factories.

By the middle of the 1760s, Britain had become the centre of cotton production, importing raw cotton from India and the United States. The raw cotton went to the mills where machines were used to spin the raw cotton into yarn, and then weave the yarn into cloth. The very first mills were powered by waterwheels, so they needed to be located close to strong-flowing rivers and streams. After the development of steam power, mill owners were able to build mills in cities – closer to a constant supply of workers and potential customers.

Before the Industrial Revolution, iron producers had to heat (smelt) the iron ore (rock) to extract the raw metal or 'pig iron' from it. Generating the necessary heat to smelt the iron ore required charcoal, but making charcoal was time-consuming and demanded large quantities of wood. Because of this, wood supplies across Britain were dwindling. In 1709, Abraham Darby, an iron producer at Coalbrookdale in Derbyshire, England, found a way to bake coal to make a substance known as coke. Coke was a new, smokeless fuel that burned much hotter than ordinary coal. Quickly, coke replaced charcoal as the fuel used to smelt iron ore. Iron foundries were established near coalfields (rather than forests), and the iron and coal industries became strongly linked.

Other innovations also made the smelting process more efficient. In 1784, iron producer Henry Cort was able to combine two processes, known as 'puddling' and 'rolling', which made the large-scale production of pig iron possible. The amount of pig iron smelted in Britain rose from 25 000 tonnes in 1728 to 60 000 tonnes in 1788. By 1796, Britain was producing 125 000 tonnes.

As production increased, new uses were found for iron. Iron utensils such as knives and forks became common, as did iron pots and pans for household kitchens. Iron was also used as a building material in factories and houses, transforming the design of buildings. For example, in 1851, London's Crystal Palace had a roof and walls made of iron frames and giant panes of glass. By this time, Britain was producing 2.25 million tonnes of pig iron, 18 times as much as in 1796. Similarly, the French put iron to use in 1889 building Gustave Eiffel's famous tower. The Eiffel Tower is an iron lattice structure created as the centrepiece of the Exposition Universelle of 1889 World's Fair in Paris, France. It is 324 metres tall – as high as an 81-storey building – and remained the tallest structure in the world until 1930.

The invention of the steam engine revolutionised manufacturing and transport, and was later used to generate electricity. Coal supplies were vital to fuel the Industrial Revolution, and the ever-increasing demand for coal led to the opening of new coal mines and the deepening of older mines. Deeper mines in turn required better pumping systems to keep water from flooding lower levels. Two inventors, Thomas Savery around 1698 and Thomas Newcomen around 1710, developed early steam engines to pump water from mines.

While repairing a Newcomen steam engine, engineer James Watt realised that he could greatly increase its efficiency. Watt did not invent the steam engine but in 1769, he developed an improved version that was more practical and powerful. In 1775, Watt formed a partnership with Matthew Boulton to manufacture new steam engines. Over the next 25 years, their firm manufactured almost 500 steam engines. They were used not only in the mining industry, but also in cotton-spinning factories, flour mills, breweries, and sugar cane crushing mills around the country.

Questions 1–6

Do the following statements agree with the information given in the Reading Passage?

Write:

TRUE *if the statement agrees with the information*
FALSE *if the statement contradicts the information*
NOT GIVEN *if there is no information on this*

1 Factory workers were initially all very skilful.

2 Cotton producers stopped using specialist workers.

3 Conditions for cotton growers were poor.

4 The location of iron producers remained near forests.

5 Steam engines were first developed for energy production.

6 Iron changed how buildings looked.

Questions 7–12

Classify the following descriptions 7–12 from the text as relating to:

A Cotton

B Iron

C Steam.

List of Descriptions

7 These factories moved to urban locations.

8 Became used in a wider range of products.

9 The basic material was bought from abroad.

10 This engine was developed to support another industry.

11 Two techniques were used together to increase production.

12 One engineer made these simpler and stronger.

Question 13

*Choose the correct letter **A**, **B**, **C** or **D**.*

Which of the following is the most suitable title for the Reading Passage?

A Working conditions in the Industrial Revolution

B The connections between industries

C Significant inventions of the Industrial Revolution

D The Industrial Revolution and the importance of Britain

Language focus 2: Habit in the past + Adverbs of frequency

(G) Grammar reference on page 220 of the Student's Book.

1 Look at sentences **1–5**. Is the use of *would/used to* correct? Why/Why not?

  1 My mother used to work but she doesn't now.

  2 That building would be a cinema.

  3 The company would be successful.

  4 Many children would practise their pronunciation every day.

  5 Some jobs used to be done by hand.

2 Number these adverbs from most (**1**) to least (**7**) frequent.

never   occasionally   always   frequently
usually   hardly ever   rarely

3 Complete the sentences with an adverb from the box.

never	occasionally	always	hardly ever	usually

1 He won't be on time. Nick is _____ late, every single time I meet him.

2 He _____ takes the train to work, but most of the time he drives.

3 They _____ played computer games when they were young. They weren't invented then.

4 I _____ used to play football in the evenings. The only time I didn't was when it rained.

5 We _____ ate out. We would just once or twice a year.

1 Look at the following Task 2 question and then answer questions **1–3** below.

WRITING TASK 2

You should spend about 40 minutes on this task.

Write about the following topic:

Some people believe computer and mobile phone technology has changed the way we communicate positively while others feel it has had a negative impact on communication with others.

Discuss both these views and give your own opinion.

Give reasons for your answer and include any relevant examples from your own knowledge or experience.

Write at least 250 words.

1 What is the topic you need to cover?

2 What are the advantages and disadvantages you need to look at?

3 In addition to the two sides of the argument, what else do you need to give?

2 Decide if each of the following arguments are an advantage (**+**) or a disadvantage (**–**). Add your own examples to each one.

	Argument	+ or –	Examples
1	Wider connection with more people.		
2	Quicker methods of communication.		
3	Face-to-face conversations happen less.		
4	Parent and child relationships might not be as strong.		

3 Look at the introduction in the sample answer in exercise 4 and match the sentences **a–c** to the functions **1–3** below.

1 Paraphrase of the main question.

2 General statement on the topic.

3 Opinion of the author.

4 Read the sample answer below and find the linking words which are used to introduce **1–6** below.

1 an example   3 results   5 purpose

2 a reason   4 additional information   6 contrast

a Technology has dramatically changed the way we communicate. **b** While some people believe this has opened up opportunities to communicate more widely, others feel that it limits the ways we communicate and may affect relationships. **c** Personally, I believe that technology has largely enhanced communication between people.

While technology has increased the ways we can communicate, some of these ways are arguably not positive developments. For instance, the majority of online communication is anonymous and consequently this is open to abuse. Similarly, it is often much easier for miscommunication to occur in methods such as emails than it is in traditional face-to-face exchanges when we can see if someone is confused or offended and so can reduce any negative feelings quickly.

Although there are many disadvantages to using technology to communicate, there are also many positives. The invention of the telephone allowed people to communicate with others outside a limited geographic area, and now anyone with a mobile phone is contactable from anywhere. Furthermore, people are able to connect much faster now than with previous traditional methods of communication such as the postal system. Therefore, it is much easier to maintain contact with a larger group of friends and to not lose touch with people over periods of time.

In conclusion, while technology has had some negative effects on our lives in the way we communicate with others, these are largely outweighed by the positives because technology has made the world feel smaller and people feel closer together. Ultimately, I feel this has a positive effect on the way we communicate.

5 Complete the alternative sample answer paragraph below with the linking words in the box.

however	because	for example	such as
moreover	in order to	as a result	

Technology has enhanced communication in many ways, **1** _____ , some people feel it has negatively affected the way we communicate. **2** _____ , face-to-face communication happens less **3** _____ people spend so much time using methods such as messaging to engage with others. **4** _____ , this may be affecting relationships **5** _____ those between parents and children. **6** _____ minimise the effects of technology on these relationships, parents need to engage in the methods used by younger people. **7** _____ , parents may find this enhances the relationship with their children.

6 Now write your own answer for the Task 2 question.

3 Thrill seekers

Vocabulary: Sports

Wordlist on page 212 of the Student's Book.

1 Use the place and equipment clues about different sports to complete the crossword.

Across

2 This sport happens in a ring and the competitors use gloves.

4 To do this sport, a boat pulls someone on skis across water.

8 People lift weights in the gym to get stronger.

Down

1 This sport is played on a pitch with two goals and a round ball.

3 An Olympic pool is 50m long. Races are between 50m and 10km. People use four main strokes – breaststroke, backstroke, butterfly and freestyle.

5 When taking part in this event, athletes use shoes with spikes to help them go faster round the track.

6 Players hit a small ball against a wall using their rackets to play this sport.

7 For this sport, players use clubs to get a small ball in a hole on a course.

2 Complete sentences **1–9** using words from the box.

motor	water	racket	winter	outdoor
combat	equestrian	indoor	team	table

1 _____ sports such as skiing and snowboarding usually happen down a hill.

2 Kick boxing and karate are examples of _____ sports in which people fight.

3 Horse and rider have to work together in _____ events, which include dressage, showjumping and endurance.

4 Formula 1 is the world's most popular _____ sport.

5 _____ sports, such as skiing, surfing and wind surfing, are often more popular in warmer countries.

6 Some _____ sports, such as real tennis, are hundreds of years old.

7 _____ sports are affected by the weather whereas _____ sports are not.

8 'Ping pong' is an alternative name for what is probably the most famous _____ sport.

9 Different individuals have to work together to win a game in _____ sports. People playing in the different positions on the pitch or field need to pull together.

Listening
Section 3

 1.3　**SECTION 3**　*Questions 21–30*

Questions 21–26

Complete the notes below.

*Write **NO MORE THAN TWO WORDS AND/OR A NUMBER** for each answer.*

Sports psychology

• Studying the impact of exercise on
  21 ....

• Study involved **22** ....
  participants

• Group 1 necessary to **23** .... other groups against.

• Group 2 went **24** .... twice a week.

• Group 3 participated in **25** .... sports.

• The majority of Group 4 did either **26** .... or climbing.

Questions 27–30

Complete the table below.

*Write **NO MORE THAN TWO WORDS AND/OR A NUMBER** for each answer.*

Results of the study

Group	Impact
Group 1	Had **27** .... on how participants felt
Group 2	Demonstrated a **28** .... fall in stress levels
Group 3	Showed the **29** .... in stress levels
Group 4	The results **30** .... a lot between different individuals.

Language focus 1: Adjectives with prepositions

Ⓖ Grammar reference on page 220 of the Student's Book.

1 Complete the sentences with the correct preposition from the box.

> on   to (x2)   about (x3)   in   with   of (x2)

1 I'm not really interested _____ team sports. I prefer individual sports.

2 I get bored _____ doing the same exercises in the gym every time. I like variety.

3 I'm keen _____ doing new things. I want to try a bungee jump!

4 She's fond _____ doing nothing. She's very lazy!

5 They are passionate _____ climbing. Every holiday is a climbing one.

6 He's capable _____ running a marathon in under three hours.

7 They are enthusiastic _____ winter sports. They especially love snowboarding.

8 I'm addicted _____ football on my computer. I can't stop playing them.

9 I'm fanatical _____ motor sports. I love watching them and doing them.

10 I'm indifferent _____ running. I don't love it or hate it.

Word building: Adjectives ending in *-ing/-ed*

1 Put the words in brackets into the correct form.

1 The race was the most _____ of my life. (challenge)

2 He was _____ to take part but winning was the most _____ thing. (excite x2)

3 I'm _____ by winning not by taking part. (motivate)

4 They were _____ by his time in qualifying. (amaze)

5 What do you find _____ about exercise? (dissatisfy)

6 Which sport do you find the most _____ ? (thrill)

2 Complete the sentences with the correct form of an adjective in the box.

> bore   tire   astonish   encourage   worry

1 I was _____ by her motivating comments. They really made me want to try harder.

2 Many people find running really _____ . I'm exhausted after just a kilometre.

3 Many doctors find people's lack of exercise _____ . It is one of their biggest concerns.

4 The team was _____ by her time. She finished in 3 hours 28 minutes and her target was 3 hours 31 minutes.

5 I'm naturally talented but I get _____ practising. Doing the same thing again and again doesn't motivate me at all.

Reading
Questions 1–13

READING PASSAGE

*You should spend about 20 minutes on **Questions 1–13**, which are based on the Reading Passage below.*

A Wingsuit jumping, for the uninitiated, is a little like transforming yourself into a human flying squirrel: the suit has parachute-like flaps of fabric under the arms and between the legs that allow the wearer to 'fly' along with the wind. It's a form of BASE jumping – BASE standing for building, antenna, span and Earth (as in the broad categories of very high things from which one can jump) – which is in itself incredibly risky, to phrase it mildly. One recent study led by the University of Colorado School of Medicine in Denver, USA, found, for example, that 72 percent of the 106 BASE jumpers interviewed had witnessed the death or catastrophic injury of a fellow jumper.

B So it makes sense to think that people who engage in these activities are taking foolish risks purely for the exhilaration of it all. But this isn't an accurate depiction of the individuals Doctor Eric Brymer, a psychologist at Queensland University of Technology in Brisbane, Australia, has encountered in more than a decade of studying experienced extreme athletes. On the contrary, Brymer said his work has suggested that many extreme athletes are the opposite of impulsive; not only are they careful and thoughtful planners, but they actually avoid thrill-seekers 'like the plague,' he said.

C When he began his work, he explained, most of the scientific literature on psychology and extreme sports linked the activity to a certain set of characteristics, 'and not very good ones at that – thrill-seeking, hedonism, that they were doing this because they liked risk.' And yet, none of these things accurately described the people he'd met at the outdoor adventure company where he worked while in grad school. As he looked into it further, he found that the bulk of the research up to that point had been done on teenagers and young adults, who tend to be high in impulsivity and poor decision-making, anyway.

D But when he conducted research specifically on experienced extreme-sports enthusiasts, he found little evidence that participants are reckless, or have some kind of Freudian death wish. Instead, Brymer has found that 'older' extreme athletes – as in those who are past their mid-20s – exercise deep care in equal proportion to the high risk involved. 'A lot of these people are highly intelligent people, methodological and systematical,' Brymer said. Those he's interviewed don't take one spontaneous trip to the outdoor clothing store REI and then jump off a cliff; rather, they spend years studying the environment and the mechanics of, for example, parachutes, before taking any action, 'in order to make it as safe as it possibly can be.' If the approach is more thoughtful for these athletes than the rest of us might suspect, so are the motivations that drive them to extreme sports in the first place. They're not just seeking an adrenaline rush, Brymer said: rather, what keeps many of them coming back is something akin to the flow-like state achieved through mindful meditation, one in which 'you're so in the moment that everything else drops away. You're focused on the here and now.'

E Dean Potter, a famous BASE jumper, once described it this way to sports channel ESPN: 'My vision is sharper, and I'm more sensitive to sounds, my sense of balance and the beauty all around me. ... Something sparkles in my mind, and then nothing else in life matters,' he said. Athletes interviewed by Brymer have expressed similar sentiments. 'The activity itself enables experiences that are beyond the everyday,' Brymer said. 'People talk about their senses being alive, about being able to see things much more clearly. It gives them a glimpse of what it means to be human, as in the capacities they have that we don't tap into in everyday life.' Another common misconception about extreme athletes is that they must have a weaker fear response than the rest of us, who might feel woozy just watching a video of Potter slack-lining in a Yosemite mountain range. 'People assume because you're doing things like BASE jumping, you have no fear,' Brymer said. 'In reality, fear is an important part of the experience.' It isn't about the absence of fear, or ignoring it when the feeling does creep in – rather, it's about learning to *use* that feeling.

F People tend to divide emotions into 'good' and 'bad', and the unpleasant anxiety of fear means it gets placed in the 'bad' category. But that's probably not the best way to think about the feeling. Fear wakes you up, making you more alert to the potential threats or things that could go wrong – all things that are very useful in a potentially dangerous situation. Brymer has interviewed BASE jumpers who say they don't like to jump with people who aren't afraid. If, when standing at the edge of a cliff, the jumper gets a little scared, this becomes a time to check in with the preparation work: their physical readiness, the environmental conditions, the equipment itself. If something isn't quite right – if the wind isn't blowing correctly, for instance – the seasoned extreme athlete will stop and come back another time.

G But if, after ticking through that mental list, everything checks out, it's time to push past that fear. 'There seems to be a link between that experience of fear and being able to move through it with the proper knowledge and expertise and training,' Brymer said. 'Instead of fear stopping them, it gets turned into this way of saying, *Okay, I need to really pay attention and be serious here.*' The presence of fear is, counterintuitively, what ultimately gives athletes 'the ability to move through fear ... it's part of what allows them to have these experiences.'

Questions 1–6

The Reading Passage has seven paragraphs, **A–G**.

Which paragraph contains the following information?

NB You may use any letter more than once.

1 people's views of extreme athletes do not match the reality

2 experienced jumpers research a jump in great detail

3 jumpers feel more alive and powerful

4 early research into the personality of extreme sports people did not look at a wide range of people

5 jumping helps people live in the moment

6 other participants see jumpers die

Questions 7–12

Do the following statements agree with the information in the Reading Passage?

Write:

> **TRUE**   *if the statement agrees with the information*
> **FALSE**   *if the statement contradicts the information*
> **NOT GIVEN** *if there is no information on this*

7 Wingsuit jumping is very different to BASE jumping.

8 All people who enjoy extreme sports make quick and risky decisions.

9 Poor decision-making is connected with younger people.

10 Extreme sports athletes are physically fit.

11 Extreme sports athletes do not suffer from fear.

12 There are lots of extreme sports videos online.

Question 13

*Choose the correct letter **A**, **B**, **C** or **D**.*

Which of the following is the most suitable title for the Reading Passage?

A Addicted to fear

B A history of extreme sports

C Controlling fear positively

D The death of a BASE jumper

Language focus 2: Comparison

(G) Grammar reference on page 221 of the Student's Book.

1 Complete the sentences with the comparative or superlative form of a word from the box below.

good	bad	noisy	difficult
stressful	popular	dangerous	cheap

1 *Star Wars* is _____ film series ever. It has made billions of dollars at the box office and through merchandise.

2 Bees are _____ than sharks. In the USA, more people die every year from a bee sting than a shark attack.

3 The Golden Raspberries Awards are for _____ films and actors. Most winners do not collect the award – no one likes to be told they are not very good.

4 One of _____ places to live in any country is near an airport.

5 It is _____ to play lots of sports from a young age rather than specialising. People who focus on one sport from a young age often get demotivated.

6 The entrance exam to Oxford University is often called _____ test in the world. It's impossible to revise for.

7 When exploring a city, it's often _____ to go on a walking tour than a bus tour. You could save up to fifty per cent of your money.

8 Being a surgeon is one of _____ jobs in the world. There is a lot of pressure when saving someone's life.

2 Rewrite the sentences using a noun instead of an adjective.

Example:

With more people taking it up, tennis is far more popular than it used to be.
With more people taking it up, tennis enjoys more popularity than it used to.

1 It's more difficult to find places to do extreme sports than regular sports.

2 Many people find running long distances more challenging than running short distances.

3 I find playing sports more interesting than watching them.

4 Which sports do you find the most motivating?

5 People want to be more thrilled by sports now than they did in the past.

6 I'm more inspired by effort than success.

7 What do you get most irritated by in sports?

8 I get more annoyed doing team sports than doing individual activities.

1 Look at the following Task 1 question and answer questions **1–5** below.

WRITING TASK 1

You should spend about 20 minutes on this task.

> *The table below shows the changes in participation levels in various sports in the USA between 2010 and 2014 for people aged between 18 and 34.*
> *Summarise the information by selecting and reporting the main features, and make comparisons where relevant.*

Write at least 150 words.

Sport	2010	2014
Baseball	3.8 million	2.2 million
Basketball	9 million	7.8 million
Hiking	12 million	14 million
Running	15 million	18 million
Softball	4 million	2.5 million
Swimming	13 million	10.5 million
Weightlifting	13.5 million	13.3 million
Yoga	9 million	12 million
Total	**79.3 million**	**80.3 million**

1 How many sports does it compare?

2 Which sports saw an increase in popularity?

3 Which sports saw the biggest increase in popularity?

4 Which sports saw a drop in popularity?

5 Which sport saw the biggest fall in popularity?

2 Look at sentences **1–6** below and decide whether the information about the table is True or False.

1 The number of people playing basketball fell from 3.8 million to 2.2 million.

2 The number of people taking part in hiking has risen.

3 In general, team sports are becoming more popular.

4 All individual sports have shown an increase in the number of people taking part.

5 Running and yoga have both increased by 3 million.

6 The numbers taking part in weightlifting remain unchanged.

3 Rewrite the sentences in exercise 2 which give false and not given information to make them true.

4 Read the model answer below and <u>underline</u> the comparative and superlative words.

> The table compares the number of 18 to 34 year old Americans participating in various sports in 2010 and 2014. Overall, the number of sports with increasing participation is equal to the number of sports with declining interest. Running is still the most popular activity, and the least popular is still baseball, however, the numbers have changed significantly. Generally speaking, people find team sports less interesting than individual activities. Baseball, basketball and softball all have between 1.2 and 1.6 million fewer participants. People are also much less inspired by swimming in 2014 than 2010. The one sport that showed little change was weightlifting. The table shows that the sports which people were more motivated to take part in in 2014 were running, hiking and yoga. All three sports had an additional 2 to 3 million individuals taking them up in the four year period. In total there are 1 million more people active in these sports.

5 Rewrite the following sentences from the model answer using a noun.

1 Generally speaking, people find team sports less interesting than individual activities.

2 People were also much less inspired by swimming in 2014 than 2010.

3 The table shows that the sports which people were more motivated to take part in in 2014 were running, hiking and yoga.

6 Match the synonyms in the box to the <u>underlined</u> words and phrases **1–6** in the overview sentence below.

the range of sporting activities	the same as	in general
numbers of people taking part	levels of engagement	falling

> ¹<u>Overall</u>, ²<u>the variety of sports</u> with increasing ³<u>participation</u> is ⁴<u>equal to</u> the number of sports with ⁵<u>declining</u> ⁶<u>interest</u>.

7 Rewrite sentences **1–3** below using the words and phrases in the box. Make any necessary changes.

amount	stayed the same	large decrease	the main pattern	rise	taking part
demonstrate	group	dramatic	individuals	on their own	generally

1 The general trend shows exercise levels remaining fairly constant.

2 Overall, the participation in team sports has shown a marked decline.

3 There has been a significant increase in the number of people doing individual sports.

8 Write your own answer for the Task 1 question.

Vocabulary 1: General nouns

Wordlist on page 212 of the Student's Book

1 Cross out the adjectives that do not collocate with the nouns in italic.

	a	**b**	**c**	
1	main	likely	perfect	*cause*
2	burning	growing	serious	*problem*
3	excellent	imaginative	golden	*opportunity*
4	insurmountable	political	special	*event*
5	burning	golden	controversial	*issue*
6	festive	state	unfavourable	*occasion*
7	dangerous	difficult	false	*situation*
8	effective	memorable	perfect	*solution*
9	adverse	favourable	good	*impression*
10	adverse	trying	festive	*circumstances*

2 Complete the sentences with words from the box.

effective solution	good impression	state occasion
golden opportunity	growing problems	likely cause

1 CO_2 emissions are the _____ of global warming.

2 It's important to make a _____ in a job interview.

3 This is a _____ for governments to reduce poverty levels.

4 The new prime minister was introduced at a _____ to celebrate political ties.

5 Obesity is an increasing problem. One _____ could be a tax on sugary foods.

6 An increasing population is causing _____ with food shortages.

🎧 1.4 **SECTION 4** *Questions 31–40*

Questions 31–37

Complete the notes below.

*Write **NO MORE THAN THREE WORDS AND/OR A NUMBER** for each answer.*

The impact and opportunities of aviation

Historical background

- First commercial flight was in 1914. 100 years later
  31 ....
  were flying every year

- Early flights were more connected with **32** ....
  than trade or leisure travel

- First commercial plane could have
  33 .... on board

- Because of the air at high altitudes people used to feel **34** ....

- Plane production grew massively from the year **35** ....

- Jet engines were designed by a British man but the **36** ....
  made the initial jet aircraft

- 1969 saw the start of the modern plane industry. The Boeing 747 was the first plane with more than one aisle, and it had two levels. It was **37** ....
  larger than previous jets

The Benoist XIV was an early bi-plane or 'flying boat' built in 1913 in America

Questions 38–40

*Choose **THREE** letters, A–F.*

Which **THREE** of the following impacts on society are mentioned?

A Transportation of goods

B Cheap flights

C Access to medical facilities

D Competition with other transport methods

E Reduced environmental impact

F Other ways CO_2 is produced

Language focus: Countable and uncountable nouns

Ⓖ Grammar reference on page 221 of the Student's Book.

1 Complete the sentences with words from the box.

bottles	burglaries	cash	chairs	crime
furniture	fruit	goods	luggage	magazines
media	merchandise	shirts	suitcases	

1 In Germany, they encourage recycling old glass _____ by giving people a small amount of _____ .

2 Due to the popularity of the internet, _____ and other traditional print _____ have fewer readers.

3 _____ rates, in particular _____ , tend to increase during difficult economic times.

4 _____ , such as _____ , are often not grown locally but are imported.

5 _____ , including _____ and other clothing, are often made cheaply. As a result people buy new things to wear every year.

6 _____ , such as _____ , tables and desks, are often not made from wood anymore. Many are made from plastic that cannot be recycled.

7 The more _____ people take on holiday, such as handbags and _____ , the greater their carbon footprint is.

2 (Circle) the uncountable nouns and underline the countable nouns in the box in exercise 1.

3 Rewrite sentences **1–7** below, so that they have the same meaning. Use the words from the box.

suggestions	cash	~~machinery~~	social media
crime	accomodation	opportunities	litter

Example:

Machines are doing more jobs people used to do.
Machinery is doing more and more jobs people used to do.

1 New flats are often smaller than older ones.

2 Coins and notes are being used less and less as we use contactless payments more.

3 Burglaries and robberies have been declining in America since the 90s.

4 Twitter and Instagram are now popular advertising methods for companies.

5 The chance for greater cultural understanding has increased with globalisation.

6 Bottles and cans in slums are seen as an opportunity by some local people to make money.

7 Advice about a healthier diet does not seem to change people's behaviour.

4 Tick the sentences that are grammatically correct. Change the sentences that are grammatically incorrect.

1 Public transports is often unreliable and expensive.

2 Password details should always be protected.

3 Nowadays, businesses is done with less and less face-to-face contact.

4 Moneys paid to pensioners is decreasing in relation to the cost of living.

5 Technological waste is a growing problem in Africa.

6 Equipments like computers develop at an increasingly rapid rate.

Reading
Questions 1–14

READING PASSAGE

*You should spend about 20 minutes on **Questions 1–14**, which are based on the Reading Passage below.*

Make your own opportunities

Are we born lucky or do we make our own luck? Some people often feel that other people get all of the luck and that they never have good fortune. However, more and more studies have found that people make their own good fortune and bad fortune. It seems that lucky events actually don't just happen by chance.

A number of inventions have arguably happened by accident including the microwave, vaccinations, X-rays, and penicillin. The people working in these areas may not have been intending to create their invention, but they had the knowledge and skills to see the potential in their discovery. When a piece of scientific equipment accidently melted the food in Percy Spencer's pocket it still took a creative and intelligent mind to make the leap to produce a microwave. Perhaps luck happens to some people more than others for a deeper reason.

Researchers at University College London are trying to find out what that reason is. The SerenA project asked people to post their stories on a website called serendipitystories.com. The word 'serendipity' can be defined as a chance encounter or accident that results in a happy, and sometimes life-changing experience. The stories range from people finding the love of their life by chance to a 91-year-old woman fulfilling her dream of riding a motorbike after a conversation in a café. Apart from reading interesting good luck stories, what did the researchers discover?

The team at UCL analysed all of these stories and found some interesting results. 'By looking for patterns, we've found that serendipity is more than an accident,' says Dr Stephan Makri. All of the people had two things in common. Firstly, all the stories did obviously contain an element of luck. However, more importantly the people spotted the opportunity and acted on it.

Richard Wiseman, a psychologist, researcher and author agrees with these findings. During his research he conducted a number of studies that lead him to a similar conclusion. In one such study he asked people to read a newspaper and to count the number of photos. In the middle of the paper he had placed a message that read 'Stop counting – there are 43 photographs in this newspaper.' 'It was staring everyone in the face, but the unlucky people tended to miss it and the lucky people spotted it,' says Wiseman.

So what causes unlucky people to fail to spot or take these opportunities? Wiseman would argue that unlucky people are usually tenser than lucky people. This increased level of anxiety leads to poor concentration and noticing skills. Consequently, unlucky people fail to notice the opportunity presented to them. However, all is not lost. We are not born lucky or unlucky. After more than ten years of research he concluded that it is actually possible for people to increase the amount of luck they have in their lives.

So how can we make ourselves luckier? For a long time people have believed in the power of superstition. From lucky numbers to touching wood to not walking under a ladder, there are many things that people believe increase or decrease their chances of good fortune. Unfortunately, the evidence is mixed as to whether superstitions actually work or not. Scientists at the University of Cologne found that carrying a good luck charm did seem to increase people's fortune. They found that people with superstitious beliefs were often calmed by their good luck charm and that this increased level of calmness may result in better performance. However, Richard Wiseman would argue that it is based on outdated and inaccurate thinking.

It seems that one way to increase your luck in life is to not be predictable. Unlucky people tend to love routine and become stressed when the routine is broken. Lucky people on the other hand are always looking for variety and to change their life. People who have very routine lives quickly use up the opportunities that are presented to them. Always doing the same things with the same people in the same place will not present many new avenues of opportunity. New and random experiences present people with unexpected opportunities from which luck may come.

The way we deal with lucky and unlucky events also varies from person to person. In particular, lucky and unlucky people react to and deal with unlucky events in very different ways. In his experiments Wiseman found that lucky people tend to look at the bad event and imagine how much worse the event could have been. Whereas, unlucky people tend to feel desperately unlucky that this event happened to them. As a result it means that fortunate people tend to be much more positive thinking about the future. This positivity decreases their anxiety and consequently means that they are likely to continue to be lucky.

So can people be taught to be luckier? If we break our daily routines, or learn how to react more positively to bad news, can we actually increase the levels of luck in our lives? Wiseman spent a month with his participants trying to train them to learn various techniques and the results were quite startling. Eighty per cent of people felt happier, more satisfied and luckier in life. Some volunteers went from feeling incredibly unlucky in life to feeling very fortunate, others found partners and some were promoted at work. All of these events arguably happened because the participants had taken control of their own luck. It seems luck is simply a state of mind.

Questions 1–9

*Complete the summary (**Questions 1–9**) using the list of words, **A–Q**, below.*

Why are some people lucky?

Lucky inventions are not **1** .... occurrences. The people had the

2 .... to see what their invention could do. SerenA wanted to analyse lucky,

3 .... stories. They found that people are fortunate but the key is how they

4 .... to the opportunity. Richard Wiseman found the **5** .... In his

experiment some unlucky people did not find the **6** .... They failed because

unlucky people are usually more **7** .... and they are unable to **8** ....

Fortunately, we can **9** .... the luck we have.

A positive	**B** unusual	**C** focus	**D** change
E chance	**F** luck	**G** closed	**H** intelligence
I live	**J** answer	**K** reason	**L** note
M respond	**N** stressed	**O** angry	**P** same **Q** want

Questions 10–14

Do the following statements agree with the claims of the writer in the Reading Passage?

Write:

YES   *if the statement agrees with the claims of the writer*

NO   *if the statement disagrees with the claims of the writer*

NOT GIVEN *if it is impossible to say what the writer thinks about this*

10 Superstitions clearly do not work.

11 A fixed daily habit leads to good luck.

12 Reacting positively to bad luck has a long-term impact.

13 Bad incidents lead to bad luck in the future.

14 People can influence luck.

Vocabulary 2: Developing ideas

1 Underline the **TWO** words that are similar in each pair of sentences.

1 The rise in levels of unemployment is alarming. It's particularly frightening for young people.

2 The low standards in education are shocking. It has stunned many parents in society.

3 Crime is increasing worldwide. Unfortunately this is a growing problem.

4 Seeing a quick change can be motivating. It can encourage people to continue.

5 I have a satisfying job. It's pleasing when I see the results.

6 Unhealthy foods are often very tempting. Since they are so appealing they are consumed too frequently.

7 The damage being done to the environment is worrying. The most troubling thing is the continued rise in the levels of pollution.

2 Complete the sentences with the adjective form of the words in the box.

satisfy	worry	motivate	grow

1 Children often want unrealistic careers. One of the _____ factors for them is the luxurious lifestyle on offer.

2 The divide between rich and poor is a _____ concern for many people.

3 Increasing inactivity in patients is a _____ trend for many doctors.

4 Having experiences such as holidays with other people is more _____ than buying more goods.

3 Continue the second sentence in **1–6** below using an adjective with a similar meaning.

Example: The Literary Festival was really interesting. It *was <u>fascinating</u> to meet so many different writers*.

1 There are frightening levels of crime in some cities. This …

2 The number of people avoiding tax has stunned the public. These …

3 The opinions of some politicians are troubling. It …

4 It is encouraging to see the number of young people starting their own business. They …

5 The falling levels of crime were pleasing to those in charge. This …

6 Certain careers are more appealing to teenagers than others. They …

1 Look at the following Task 2 question and then answer questions **1–6** below.

WRITING TASK 2

You should spend about 40 minutes on this task.

Write about the following topic:

> *Youth unemployment is increasing in many countries in the world. What do you think are the main causes of this problem and what measures can be taken to solve it?*

Give reasons for your answer and include any relevant examples from your own knowledge or experience.

Write at least 250 words.

---

1 What is the main topic?

2 Is it a positive or negative development?

3 What two main areas do you need to focus on for the topic?

4 Can you add things from your personal life?

5 How long do you have for the task?

6 Can you write more than 250 words?

2 Match the causes **1–4** to the solutions **a–d**.

1 The main cause of youth unemployment is the increasing use of robots and technology to do basic jobs.

2 Another factor is the lack of diversity on the type of jobs available.

3 This is arguably as a result of the academic path people are choosing to take.

4 One cause is the lack of apprenticeships in many firms.

a One way to deal with this is to for people to learn a greater range of skills.

b Companies should be supported by the government to develop training schemes.

c One solution is for governments to provide financial support for industries such as manufacturing.

d Young people should be encouraged to train in skills there is a shortage in.

3 Put sentences **1–5** for this possible model answer in the correct order.

1 For instance, many manufacturing jobs and customer service jobs are now completed by computers or robots.

2 Consequently, many low-skilled jobs are now no longer available to people.

3 The main cause of youth unemployment is the increasing use of technology and the automation of basic jobs.

4 However, doing so will take time and will not help those who have been working in this area for a long time already.

5 One solution could be for people to learn a greater range of skills that cannot be replicated by technology.

4   Match the functions **a–e** to the sentences in exercise 3.

   1 Sentence 1   **a** example

   2 Sentence 2   **b** solution

   3 Sentence 3   **c** result

   4 Sentence 4   **d** concession

   5 Sentence 5   **e** main idea

5   Complete the model answer by <u>underlining</u> the correct word in *italics*.

Recent economic events have led to increased levels of unemployment in many countries. In particular, they have resulted in very high levels of youth unemployment, even as high as 50% in some countries. There are a number of reasons for this phenomenon, **1** *however/such as*, there are realistic solutions that could be employed.

Many economies are now reliant on a very limited range of jobs, for example, the UK largely employees people in service jobs. **2** *Furthermore/As a result* many jobs in the whole economy can be affected at the same time. One solution is for governments to provide financial support to make smaller sectors larger. For instance, the UK government could invest in growing its manufacturing sector.

In recent years many countries have seen increases in the number of university graduates. At the same time, there has been a fall in the number of people qualifying in traditional professions such as electricians and plumbers. **3** *Consequently/Even so*, young people should be encouraged to train in skills there is a shortage of.

4 *On the other hand/Furthermore*, companies do not often provide the level of training they once did. For example, there is a lack of apprenticeships in many firms. The government should support companies to develop training schemes. **5** *As a result/Whereas* this will develop employees with the specific knowledge and skills companies require rather than broad, generic knowledge.

In conclusion, while youth unemployment may be high there are a number of steps many countries could take to reduce these levels. In particular, training young people in the skills society requires.

6   Write your own answer for the Task 2 question.

5 The future

Language focus: Ways of looking at the future

(G) Grammar reference on page 222 of the Student's Book.

1 Match a tense **1–6** to each sentence **a–f**.

1 The present continuous

2 The future continuous

3 The present simple

4 The future perfect

5 *will*

6 *going to*

a The train leaves at 5.50.

b People will be doing very different jobs in 30 years' time.

c I'm meeting friends for coffee tonight.

d Most people will work from home in the future.

e By 2030, most jobs will have changed beyond recognition.

f I'm going to travel around Europe with friends.

2 Match the functions **a–f** to a tense in exercise 1.

a Used for intentions or plans.

b Used for fixed arrangements.

c Used for a completed action at or before a point in the future.

d Used for a situation which will be happening at a particular time in the future.

e Used for predictions or instant decisions.

f Used for events that relate to a schedule/timetable.

3 For **1–8** below, <u>underline</u> the correct form in *italics*.

1 By 2030, most people *will be using/use* driverless cars.

2 By the time people are thirty, they *will have changed/will change* jobs four or five times.

3 We *will have bought/'re going to buy* a new car.

4 The shops *are going to close/close* at 10 pm every day.

5 I *get married/will probably get married* and have children.

6 I *'m starting/will start* a new job tomorrow.

7 By 2025, most things *will be delivered/are being delivered* by drones.

8 People *will often choose/will be often choosing* not to have children.

4 Complete the sentences with the correct form of the word in brackets.

1 By tomorrow, I _____ (finish) the essay.

2 The presentation _____ (start) in ten minutes.

3 The lesson _____ (last) one hour every Monday afternoon.

4 Men and women _____ (earn) the same money by 2030.

5 We _____ (go/go) kite surfing this summer.

6 We won't need keys, remote controls or light switches. I think phones _____ (control) everything in our house.

Vocabulary 1: Adjective/Noun collocations

Wordlist on page 213 of the Student's Book.

1 Choose the correct word to complete the sentences.

1 The (indigenous/modern/dominant) people of many countries suffered at the hands of invaders.

2 The (thriving/agricultural/general) public protested about the government's decision.

3 There is a (dominant/thriving/urban) local economy which has increased salaries above the national average.

4 The historic town centre is much more attractive than the (modern/urban/general) area.

5 It is an (urban/agricultural/indigenous) region and most people work in farming.

6 Throughout the world the (urban/agricultural/indigenous) population has been increasing as more and more people move to cities.

7 The (thriving/general/governing) elite has made some unpopular decisions and is unlikely to win the next election.

8 American culture has influenced many societies around the world. Hollywood movies help make it the (dominant/general/governing) culture.

2 Complete the sentences with collocations from the box.

indigenous people	general public	thriving economy	modern area
agricultural region	urban population	governing elite	dominant culture

1 He is a good politician but not popular with the _____ . Most of the population dislikes him.

2 Many of the _____ no longer speak their own language. They have learnt the language of the people who conquered the island.

3 The _____ has become smaller as cities have grown.

4 A _____ is usually richer than a rural one.

5 The _____ is a lot less beautiful than the historical area.

6 India is a very diverse country and there is not one _____ .

7 The _____ control most of the power and wealth in the country.

8 We once had a _____ but now it is struggling. I think we'll have a recession soon.

Listening
Section 1

1.5 **SECTION 1** *Questions 1–10*

Questions 1–4

Complete the notes below.

Write **NO MORE THAN TWO WORDS AND/OR A NUMBER** *for each answer.*

Future development

Exhibition date: **1** ....

Location: **2** ....

Number of tickets booked: **3** ....

Delivery method: **4** ....

Questions 5 and 6

*Choose **TWO** letters, **A–E**.*

Which **TWO** of the following facilities will be available on the site?

A Beach

B Swimming pool

C Supermarket

D Restaurants

E Tennis court

Questions 7–10

Complete the table below.

Write **NO MORE THAN TWO WORDS AND/OR A NUMBER** *for each answer.*

Methods of transport	Nearest stop to development	Frequency	Destination	Cost
Tram	The front entrance	Every **7**	All main towns along the regional coast	**8** .... return
Bus	**9**	Every 15 minutes	Inland towns and **10**	Five euros return

Word building: Forming adjectives from nouns

Wordlist on page 213 of the Student's Book.

1 Make adjectives from the nouns in brackets using one of these three suffixes: *-al, -(i)ous*
and *-ful* . Make any necessary changes.

1 _____ sports are often popular among thrill seekers. (danger)

2 China is likely to become the most economically _____ country
in the world. (power)

3 Industrialisation continues to be _____ to the environment. (harm)

4 _____ people often want control of their future. (ambition)

5 There are _____ reasons why it isn't appropriate. (culture)

6 Solar energy has become more and more _____ . (economy)

7 Many doubt we are likely to have a _____ world in the future. (peace)

8 The internet is seen as one of the most influential _____ developments of recent
years. (technology)

2 Complete the sentences with nouns or adjectives of the words in brackets.

1 America currently has significant _____ and political _____ . (economy/power)

2 Society has undergone huge _____ changes due to the development of
_____ . (culture/technology)

3 Some people see businesses' _____ as _____ for society. (ambition/danger)

4 The breakdown in _____ talks was _____ for the region. (peace/harm)

3 Underline all the noun forms in the completed sentences in exercise 2.

Reading
Questions 1–13

READING PASSAGE

*You should spend about 20 minutes on **Questions 1–13**, which are based on the
Reading Passage below.*

A report from Public Health England in February this year found that over-65s in Britain are living longer than ever before — but we want life in our years, not just years in our lives.

Here's what our generation can hope for.

Younger skin

It's an exciting idea for those of us who seem to find a new wrinkle each morning: a wearable film applied to the face or body as a thin, transparent layer, making skin look younger. The new silicone-based polymer film, dubbed 'second skin', was developed at the Massachusetts Institute of Technology. After tests, researchers reported that it covered eye bags and wrinkles, making skin look smoother and firmer, and more elastic and springy. The product is applied as two creams, one after the other, that dry into a film and can then be peeled off and discarded

24 hours later. The treatment was co-developed with a cosmetic company and while the MIT researchers refused to speculate on when the treatment might become available, Dr Agus, who wasn't involved in the research says: 'My gut is we'll see it sometime in 2017.'

Fighting disease

Having your DNA genetically modified or 'edited' could be available within five years, says Dr Agus. Last year, biotech company Editas Medicine announced plans to become the first lab in the world to genetically edit the DNA of patients suffering from a genetic condition that prevents the normal functioning of the retina. It's possible thanks to new cutting-edge gene-editing technology Crispr, which stands for Clustered, Regularly Interspaced, Short Palindromic Repeat, a naturally occurring defence mechanism used by bacteria that the technology harnesses to erase mutated areas of DNA.

'Crispr acts like scissors to cut out defective pieces of DNA so they can be replaced with other pieces of DNA,' says Dr Agus. 'Using this technique, researchers have managed to tweak the genes in fish that affect how they age. It offers hope of finding treatments that can help us age slower and live longer.' But there are ethical concerns, says Dr Agus. 'The technology could be potentially used to control qualities such as intelligence, athleticism and beauty, and we don't know what revising the human genome to create permanent genetic modifications could mean for future generations.'

Living longer

While a bona-fide proven pill that could add years to our lives is not yet reality, it's on the way, says UCL ageing researcher Dr Alic – most likely in the form of drugs currently available for other conditions that in trials have been shown to have an anti-ageing effect. In June last year, Dr Alic's team found that fruit flies given a cancer drug lived 12 per cent longer than average and last month, another UCL team found the drug lithium – routinely prescribed for the treatment of bipolar disorder – could lead to a lifespan increased by up to 18 per cent.

Meanwhile, a medicine called rapamycin, used to suppress the immune system in transplant patients, has been shown in mice trials to prolong life by 38 per cent, and in one study last month on dogs, it improved their heart functionality. While its use as an anti-ageing drug is more than a decade off, Dr Alic explains, rapamycin has been shown in humans to help vaccine responses in the elderly. 'That's a positive effect on which we could base potential treatment,' he says. But it's no wonder drug, he says and side-effects include suppression of the immune system.

A better quality life

While we may not be able to live forever, scientists are confident that they can extend the quality of life to a much older age. Scientists now believe that it is possible to actually stop people growing old as quickly and help them live in good health well into their 110s and 120s. Although it might seem like science fiction, researchers have already proven that the diabetes drug metformin extends the life of animals, and the Food and Drug Administration in the US has now given the go ahead for a trial to see if the same effects can be replicated in humans. 'This would be the most important medical intervention in the modern era, an ability to slow ageing' says Dr Jay Olshansky, University of Illinois, Chicago. If successful, it will mean that a person in their 70s would be as biologically healthy as a 50 year old. It could usher in a new era of 'geroscience' where doctors would no longer fight individual conditions like cancer, diabetes and dementia, but instead treat the underlying mechanism – ageing. Professor Lithgow believes that, in the future, young people may be given a type of ageing 'vaccine' to slow down ageing. He believes it could have a far bigger impact on extending population lifespan than finding a cure for cancer. 'If we were to cure all cancers it would only raise life expectancy by around three years, because something else is coming behind the cancer, but if we could slow down the ageing process, you could dramatically improve how long people can live,' he said. 'We know that it is possible for handfuls of people to live to a very old age and still be physically and socially active, so clearly they carry some kind of protection in their bodies. They are essentially not ageing as quickly. If we can harness that, then everyone can achieve those lifespans.'

Questions 1–7

Complete the summary below.

Choose **NO MORE THAN TWO WORDS AND/OR A NUMBER** *from the passage for each answer.*

People want to live a longer and better quality life. The Massachusetts Institute of Technology has produced something called a **1** .... to make our skin look younger. It can be removed **2** .... one day later. Changing our DNA might be possible in **3** .... time. It works by using a protection system **4** .... use to remove weak parts. So far, scientists have used it to change how **5** .... age. It's possible this could help humans survive **6** .... It might also be used to affect **7** .... , physical ability and attractiveness.

Questions 8–11

Choose the correct letter **A, B, C** *or* **D.**

8 Anti-aging drugs

  A are already available and can add years to your life.

  B are being tested on fruit flies.

  C are likely to come from drugs we already have for treating major illnesses.

  D make people live 12 to 18% longer.

9 The medicine rapamycin

  A increases peoples' lives by 38%.

  B helps protect old people from future illnesses.

  C is a vaccine for old people.

  D has very few side-effects on people.

10 Scientists are convinced that

  A we may be able to slow down the ageing process.

  B it is possible to live forever.

  C we need good healthcare for those in their 110s and 120s.

  D we should focus on quality of life rather than extending it.

11 A trial of the drug metformin has been authorised in the US

  A to treat diabetes in animals.

  B to prove that it can extend the lifespan of animals.

  C to check if it can increase human as well as animal lifespans.

  D to test if people in their 70s are as healthy as people in their 50s.

Questions 12 and 13

Answer the questions below.

Choose **NO MORE THAN THREE WORDS** *from the passage for each answer.*

12 What do we need to combat to increase life expectancy?

13 What do some old people have in their system that others do not?

Vocabulary 2: Verbs of prediction

Wordlist on page 213 of the Student's Book.

1 Put the words in brackets into the correct form.

1 It _____ that over 50% of purchases will be made on the internet. (estimate)

2 Food shortages _____ to increase. (forecast)

3 By 2050, French _____ to be the most commonly spoken first language. (project)

4 The number of students _____ to decline in the coming years. (anticipate)

5 Japan's population _____ to fall. (expect)

6 Sales of digital cameras _____ to fall. (predict)

Writing
Task 1

1 Look at the following Task 1 question and then answer questions **1–3** below.

WRITING TASK 1

You should spend about 20 minutes on this task.

> *The pie charts below compare household spending in the UK in 1980 with predictions for 2030.*
>
> *Summarise the information by selecting and reporting the main features, and make comparisons where relevant.*

Write at least 150 words.

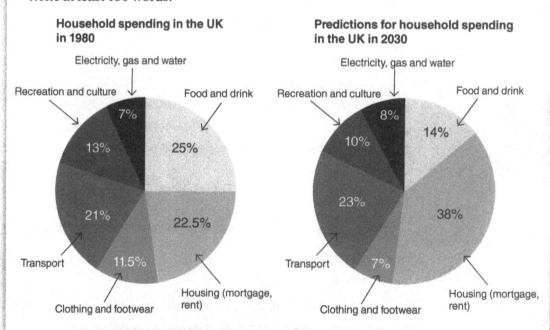

1 How many categories do you have to compare?

2 Which category is predicted to fall the most?

3 Which category is expected to rise the most?

2 Complete the sentences with relevant data from the pie charts on page 42.

1 It is estimated that the proportion of income spent on recreation will fall from _____ to _____ .

2 Food and drink accounted for _____ of household expenditure in 1980. In contrast, it is expected to be just _____ in 2030.

3 By 2030, household spending on clothing and footwear is forecast to fall to _____ .

4 Proportionally, the amount spent on _____ is projected to be the smallest change.

5 Spending on transport is anticipated to increase by _____ .

6 The cost of housing is predicted to nearly double by 2030 to _____ of household spending.

3 Put the verbs in brackets into the correct tense in the model answer.

The pie charts **1** _____ (illustrate) the expected changes in household expenditure in 2030 compared to 1980. The two most notable features **2** _____ (be) the fall in the cost of food and drink and the increase in housing costs. Spending on food and drink **3** _____ (forecast) to nearly halve in this period, falling from 25% to 14%. By contrast, it **4** _____ (anticipate) that there **5** _____ (be) a dramatic rise in housing costs from 22.5% to 38%. In comparison to these two changes, the other changes **6** _____ (predict) to be relatively small. Clothing/footwear and recreation/culture **7** _____ (project) to fall slightly, while transport and electricity, gas and water **8** _____ (expect) to increase slightly, both of which are likely to be connected.

With the significant increase in housing costs, it is clear that some areas of people's lives **9** _____ (affect). The most significant fall **10** _____ (be) in the money available for spending on food.

4 Choose the correct option to complete each sentence.

1 In 1980, food and drink accounted for 25% of the household budget (meanwhile/whereas) it is forecast to only make up 14% by 2030.

2 Three categories each accounted for over 20% of spending (while/but) the rest were all under 20% of the budget.

3 The costs of three categories are predicted to rise (but/whereas) housing is expected to rise much more than any other.

4 The cost of food and drink is projected to fall dramatically. (Meanwhile/In contrast) recreation and culture will show little change.

5 Write your own answer to the Task 1 question.

6 The fruits of nature

Vocabulary 1: Lifecycles and processes

Wordlist on page 213 of the Student's Book.

1 Read the four texts **a–d** and match them to the four processes shown in the diagrams **1–4**.

a Seeds require three factors to germinate. Firstly, they need water to swell up and for the embryo to start growing. Next, they need oxygen so that energy can be released for germination. Lastly, the process is significantly enhanced as the temperature rises.

b Frog spawn is made of thousands of floating eggs. Frogs lay so many eggs because, unlike some animals, they do not look after their eggs once laid and many get eaten by other animals. Around two weeks after being laid, a head and tail will develop inside the egg. Once out of the egg, the tadpole's back legs and then finally the front legs grow. Soon after, the tail disappears.

c Green plants absorb energy from the sun using chlorophyll in their leaves. The energy is used to react carbon dioxide with water to make a sugar called glucose. The glucose is used for respiration (the process of how plants 'breathe'), or it is changed into starch and stored. Oxygen is produced during this process.

d It is possible for plants to reproduce without flowers or fertilisation. Plants such as strawberries and potatoes use tubers or runners to produce new plants. New plants produced in this way are identical to each other and are called 'a clone'.

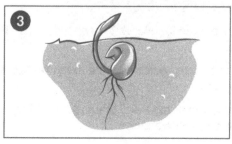
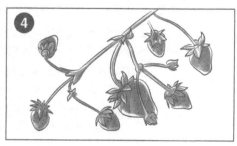

2 <u>Underline</u> the words that helped you in exercise 1.

Reading
Questions 1–14

READING PASSAGE

You should spend about 20 minutes on **Questions 1–14**, which are based on the Reading Passage below.

A brief history of chocolate

A It's hard to pin down exactly when chocolate was born, but it's clear that it was cherished from the start. For several centuries, in pre-modern Latin America, cacao beans were considered valuable enough to use as currency. One bean could be traded for a tamale (a traditional dish), while 100 beans could purchase a good turkey hen, according to a 16th-century Aztec document.

B Sweetened chocolate didn't appear until Europeans discovered the Americas and sampled the native cuisine. Legend has it that the Aztec king Montezuma welcomed the Spanish explorer Hernando Cortes with a banquet that included drinking chocolate, having tragically mistaken him for a reincarnated god instead of a conquering invader. Chocolate didn't suit the foreigners' taste buds at first – one described it in his writings as 'a bitter drink for pigs' – but once mixed with honey or cane sugar, it quickly became popular throughout Spain.

C By the 17th century, chocolate was a fashionable drink throughout Europe, believed to have nutritious and medicinal properties. But it remained largely a privilege of the rich until the invention of the steam engine made mass production possible in the late 1700s. In 1828, a Dutch chemist found a way to make powdered chocolate by removing about half the natural fat (cacao butter) from chocolate liquor, pulverizing what remained and treating the mixture with alkaline salts to cut the bitter taste. His product became known as 'Dutch cocoa,' and it soon led to the creation of solid chocolate.

D The creation of the first modern chocolate bar is credited to Joseph Fry, who in 1847 discovered that he could make a moldable chocolate paste by adding melted cacao butter back into Dutch cocoa. By 1868, a little company called Cadbury was marketing boxes of chocolate candies in England. Milk chocolate hit the market a few years later, pioneered by another name that may ring a bell – Nestlé.

E Chocolate begins with the cacao tree, which grows within 20° north and south of the Equator and thrives on a mix of hot temperatures, rain, and shade.

Each tree bears oval fruits, or pods, which are about 5–12 inches long. Each pod contains 30–50 seeds, and it's these seeds the world knows as cacao (or cocoa) beans. The tree, pod, and bean/seed are typically referred to as 'cacao', while the word 'cocoa' is reserved for the bean after it has been fermented, dried, and roasted.

F Cacao pods are ripe when they turn a vibrant yellow/orange colour. Hanging from the trunk, and largest branches, on small stems, the ripening pods are typically harvested twice per year, though they can be harvested continually. After being chopped off, the pods are opened and their seeds are removed. Each seed is about the size of an olive. The seeds (or 'beans') grow in five columns surrounded by a white pulp or pith.

G Beans are cleaned by hand, with the *baba* (sweet pulp of the inside of the bean) left on to help develop flavour. Exposed to light, the cream-coloured beans turn a purplish colour. Then they're ready for fermentation via one of two ways: the 'heap method' is popular in Africa, where beans are heaped in piles on the ground; and in Latin America, a system of cascading boxes is favoured. In both methods, beans are covered with banana leaves. During the 2–9 days of fermentation, beans begin to take on colour and some of the flavours you would recognise as 'chocolate'.

H Fermented beans must be carefully dried. They are placed either on wooden boards or bamboo mats for anywhere from 7 to 14 days under the hot sun, and are continually raked and turned over for consistent drying. Once dried, the beans are graded, packed into sacks, bundled, and checked for quality. They are then shipped and traded on the international market.

I Beans are cleaned, then roasted at low temperatures to develop flavour. Shells are separated from the nibs by a process called winnowing. Nibs are finely ground into cocoa mass or cocoa liquor, which is solid at room temperature. Placed under extremely high pressure, this paste yields two products: cocoa powder and cocoa butter.

J Cocoa mass can simply be combined with more cocoa butter and sweetener to make chocolate. The first steps are to mix, grind, and knead the various raw ingredients into a paste – a process known as conching. The chocolate is now finished and ready for final processing. To be delivered to a chocolatier, it must first be put into blocks or drops. This method requires 'tempering' – whereby chocolate is slowly brought to a certain temperature. During the tempering process, the cocoa butter reaches its most stable form; this gives well-tempered chocolate its 'snap,' shiny surface, and smoothness.

Questions 1–5

The Reading Passage has ten paragraphs, **A–J**.

Which paragraph contains the following information?

1 the original companies and people involved in making today's chocolate

2 the time when the fruit is picked

3 the changes made to chocolate by Spain

4 getting the two key products from the bean

5 when the colour and the taste first develop

Questions 6–8

Do the following statements agree with the information given in the Reading Passage?

Write:

TRUE   *if the statement agrees with the information*
FALSE   *if the statement contradicts the information*
NOT GIVEN *if there is no information on this*

6 Cacao beans were once used as money.

7 The Spanish stole cocoa from the Aztecs.

8 The Dutch added sugar to make chocolate sweet.

Questions 9–14

Complete the flow-chart below.

Choose **NO MORE THAN TWO WORDS** *from the passage for each answer.*

Stages in the production of chocolate

cacao trees grown near **9** .... in hot wet climate

↓

after harvesting, **10** .... taken out

↓

after fermentation, beans **11** .... for one or two weeks

↓

enhance the taste = beans are **12** .... in a cool heat

↓

cocoa powder and butter extracted, then the ingredients go through **13** ....

↓

finally, the chocolate is heated in a process called **14** ....

Language focus: Transitive and intransitive verbs

(G) Grammar reference on page 223, and Wordlist on page 214, of the Student's Book.

1 Complete sentences **1–6** with words from the box. Change the form if necessary. Decide whether the verbs are being used transitively or intransitively.

make collect crush occur rise emerge

1 The first plants _____ from the ground in May and June.

2 The press _____ the fruit to create the juice.

3 The sun _____ at 7 every day.

4 It _____ from recycled plastic.

5 Bees _____ nectar for their hive.

6 A full moon _____ once a month.

2 Complete the text with words from the box. More than one answer may be possible, and you may use any word more than once. Change the form as necessary.

produce	grow	cross-pollination	bear
cultivate	sprout	ripen	prune

The lifecycle of a cultivated banana tree

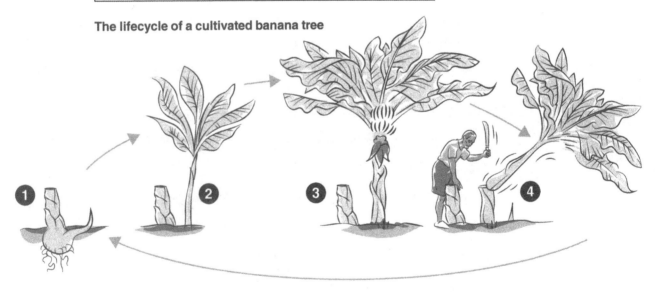

Modern banana trees aren't actually trees – they are very large herb plants that **1** _____ from wild banana trees. Thousands of years ago **2** _____ of the first banana trees produced an edible fruit. The fruit (or bananas) that the tree **3** _____ are essentially berries with a protective skin.

Banana trees don't grow from seed. Instead, shoots **4** _____ horizontally from the underground root stem. On modern banana plantations usually only one shoot is allowed to grow to form a stalk, which **5** _____ up to six leaves that can be nine feet long and two feet wide. The new tree takes about nine months to **6** _____ a bunch of bananas. Plenty of sunshine and water will cause the fruit to **7** _____ .

The mature tree then dies and is chopped down. However one sucker is allowed to **8** _____ , while all the others will be **9** _____ to ensure there is room for next year's crop.

3 Cross out the noun that does not collocate with each verb on the left.

1	prune	**a** branches	**b** trees	**c** buds
2	plant	**a** trees	**b** branches	**c** seeds
3	pollinate	**a** flowers	**b** trees	**c** buds
4	become	**a** saplings	**b** flowers	**c** seeds
5	gather	**a** fruit	**b** trees	**c** flowers
6	harvest	**a** seeds	**b** saplings	**c** fruit
7	sprout	**a** buds	**b** seeds	**c** saplings
8	bear	**a** flowers	**b** fruit	**c** trees

Vocabulary 2: Conservation

Wordlist on page 213 of the Student's Book.

1 Match the words **1–8** to the definitions **a–h**.

1	conservation	**a**	interesting places that people go to see
2	extinction	**b**	peaceful
3	sights	**c**	something that is now worse than its original state
4	view	**d**	when a plant or animal no longer exists
5	spoilt	**e**	the long term protection of a plant or animal
6	tranquil	**f**	the ability to see something from a particular place
7	spectacular	**g**	amazing
8	scenery	**h**	natural things such as trees, hills and lakes that you see in a particular place

2 Complete the sentences with words from exercise 1.

1 Some people think too much money has been spent on the _____ of pandas.

2 We went to Barcelona to see the _____ .

3 There is a _____ view from the top of the tower.

4 We had a great _____ from our balcony.

5 The _____ in the national park is stunning.

6 I enjoy walking in the mountains because it's so _____ .

7 The growth of the city _____ much of the countryside.

8 Over 1,000 species are in danger of _____ .

3 Some of the sentences below contain mistakes. Correct the incorrect sentences.

1 The mountains in the north have amazing views, stretching as far as the eye can see.

2 The walk along the coast provides some breath taking scenic.

3 There are a number of charities that are involved in the protection of animals and the conservation of the environment.

4 The skyline is domination by the volcano in the north.

Listening
Section 2

🎧 1.6 **SECTION 2** *Questions 11–20*

Questions 11–13

*Choose the correct letter, **A**, **B** or **C**.*

11 The school will develop the site from
   A September.
   B January.
   C April.

12 At first the facilities
   A will be built by older year groups.
   B will be open to all the school.
   C will be open to year one and two only.

13 If you don't want your child to take part in the TV programme
   A email the school.
   B complete the form.
   C write a letter to the school.

Questions 14–17

*Label the map opposite. Write the correct letter, **A–H**, next to Questions 14–17.*

14 Educational hut   ....

15 Bird-watching area ....

16 Treehouse   ....

17 Picnic area   ....

Woodlands Development plan

Questions 18–20

Complete the sentences below.

*Write **NO MORE THAN TWO WORDS** for each answer.*

18 Parents can help in the summer by .... to the scheme.

19 Children can take part in a competition to design the ....

20 .... can be emailed throughout the summer.

Describing sequences

Look at the following Task 1 question about a diagram which shows a process.
Then do exercises **1–5**.

WRITING TASK 1

You should spend about 20 minutes on this task.

> *The diagram below shows the process of making paper and then how recycled paper is also made.*
>
> *Summarise the information by selecting and reporting the main features, and make comparisons where relevant.*

Write at least 150 words.

Plantation to paper and paper to paper

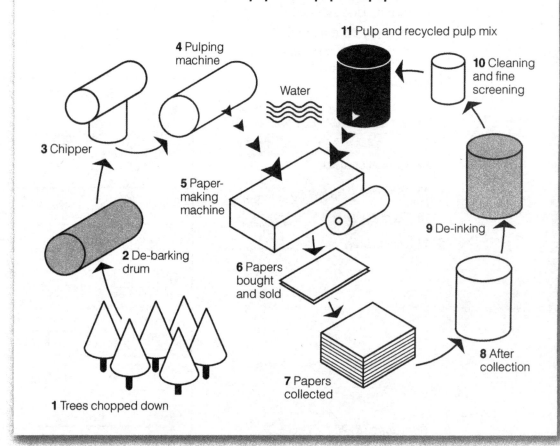

1 Trees chopped down
2 De-barking drum
3 Chipper
4 Pulping machine
5 Paper-making machine
6 Papers bought and sold
7 Papers collected
8 After collection
9 De-inking
10 Cleaning and fine screening
11 Pulp and recycled pulp mix
Water

1 Match the words in the box to as many of the steps in the process diagram above as possible.

use	process	recycle	chop down	re-process	production

2 Look at the words in the box below. Which words can be used

a in step 1?

b in any step from 2 to 10?

c in the last step?

as soon as	after	at first	before	following that	next
initially	first	when	then	finally	

3 <u>Underline</u> the linking words in **1–7**. Then put the sentences in order.

1 At first, the trees are chopped down and

2 Initially, the bark is removed

3 subsequently taken to the processing plant and put into the de-barking drum.

4 before then being put through the chipping machine.

5 Following that the chips are processed in the pulping machine to make the pulp that is turned into paper.

6 The diagram shows the process of making paper and

7 then how recycled paper is also made.

4 Match **1–7** below with a sentence or part of a sentence **a–g** to complete the process.

1 From the paper-making machine it is then

2 This paper can then be used

3 These papers are then

4 Following that, the papers are collected

5 The first step of this stage is

6 Following that,

7 Finally, the cleaned paper is then passed through the pulping process again

a to create newspapers. And the second part of the cycle begins.

b and then the recycling process can be started.

c taken to the final stage to create the product for use.

d to remove the ink from the old papers.

e the de-inked paper is then cleaned.

f sold and bought by customers.

g before then being turned back into paper.

5 Write your own answer to the Task 1 question.

Vocabulary 1: Work

Wordlist on page 214 of the Student's Book.

1 Use the clues below to complete the crossword.

Across

1 The tasks done to complete your job.

3 A profession or series of jobs you choose and spend most of your life working in.

5 A person who needs special skills, training or qualifications to do their job.

6 Something you get after completing an examination or course, e.g. High School Diploma.

7 Work you do regularly for money.

Down

2 Has the same meaning as job or profession.

4 The income from your job that enables you to live.

2 Complete the sentences using the words from exercise 1. You may need to change the form of some of the words.

1 He wants to climb the _____ ladder as quickly as possible.

2 Accountancy exams are really hard to pass. When did you _____ as an accountant?

3 Working in _____ positions such as those in accountancy, medicine, teaching and law can mean long hours but can be very rewarding.

4 I _____ in the accounting department but I hope to move to a different department next year.

5 I don't enjoy my job but it's my _____ . My family depend on the money I earn.

6 What _____ did you put on the form? Lecturer or teacher?

7 How many interviews did you have before you got the _____ ?

Reading
Questions 1–13

READING PASSAGE

*You should spend about 20 minutes on **Questions 1–13**, which are based on the Reading Passage below.*

No to 9-to-5

Sleep deprivation has been shown to have major impacts on health. Just one week with less than six hours sleep each night leads to 711 changes in how genes function. Lack of sleep impacts performance, attention, and long-term memory. It also leads to exhaustion, anxiety, frustration, anger, impulsive behaviour, weight gain, risk-taking, high blood pressure, lower immunity, stress and a raft of mental health conditions. Forcing staff to start work before 10am is tantamount to torture and is making employees ill, exhausted and stressed, an Oxford University academic has claimed. Before the age of 55, the circadian rhythms of adults are completely out of sync with normal 9-to-5 working hours, which poses a 'serious threat' to performance, mood and mental health.

Dr Paul Kelley, of Oxford University, said there was a need for a huge societal change to move work and school starting times to fit with the natural body clock of humans. Experiments studying circadian rhythms have shown that the average 10-year-old will not start focusing properly for academic work before 8.30am. Similarly, a 16-year-old should start at 10am for best results and university students should start at 11am. Dr Kelley believes that simply moving school times could raise grades by 10 per cent. He was formerly a head teacher at Monkseaton Middle School, in North Tyneside, where he changed the school start day from 8.30am to 10am and found that the number of top grades rose by 19 per cent.

Similarly, companies who force employees to start work earlier are also likely to be hurting their output, while storing up health problems for staff. Dr Paul Kelley said work and school starting times should fit with the natural body clock. 'This is a huge society issue,' Dr Kelley told the British Science Festival in Bradford. 'Staff should start at 10am. You don't get back to (the 9am) starting point till 55. Staff are usually sleep-deprived. We've got a sleep-deprived society.'

'It is hugely damaging on the body's systems because you are affecting physical, emotional and performance systems in the body. Your liver and your heart have different patterns and you're asking them to shift two or three hours. This is an international issue. Everybody is suffering and they don't have to. We cannot change our 24-hour rhythms. You cannot learn to get up at a certain time. Your body will be attuned to sunlight and you're not conscious of it because it reports to the hypothalamus, not sight.'

Prof Russell Foster, a neuroscientist from the University of Oxford, said lack of sleep is damaging the health of the nation, with too many early risers trying to function with brain skills badly affected. The comments follow studies which suggest that working night shifts speeds up the ageing process, and is linked to increasing risks

of cancer, heart disease and type two diabetes. In 2010, a major study found that people who slept for less than six hours each night were 12 per cent more likely to die prematurely – before the age of 65 – than those who slept the recommended six to eight hours a night. The team from the University of Warwick and Federico II University Medical School in Naples analysed 16 studies involving a total of 1.3 million people.

Neuroscientists say teens are biologically predisposed to go to sleep at around midnight and not feel fully awake and engaged until around 10am. Dr Kelley said that almost all students were losing around 10 hours of sleep a week because they were forced to get up too early. 'Just by changing the school start time you can improve quality of life for whole generations of children,' he added. 'There are major societal problems that are being caused by that. But the opportunities are fantastic. We have an opportunity here to do something that would benefit millions of people on Earth.'

Tens of thousands of children are starting school at 10am in a ground-breaking experiment by Oxford University to prove that later classes can improve exam results. GCSE students from more than 100 schools across England will take part in the four-year project based on scientific evidence which suggests teenagers are out of sync with traditional school. The team is hoping to publish findings in 2018.

A Department of Education spokesman said: 'We have given all schools the freedom to control the length of the school day because they are best placed to know what's best for their communities. Allowing more time for supervised study and extra-curricular activities has been shown to benefit disadvantaged pupils in particular by giving them access to purposeful, character-building activities, which is why we are helping schools offer a longer day.'

There are many ways you can improve your sleep. Buy heavy curtains – anything to keep the room where you sleep dark. Light suppresses melatonin, the hormone that relaxes your body. It's also important to establish a regular sleep pattern – going to bed and waking up at roughly the same time each day helps enormously. Your body and mind will feel much better for it.

Questions 1–7

Complete the notes below.

*Choose **NO MORE THAN TWO WORDS AND/OR A NUMBER** from the passage for each answer.*

Impact of poor sleep

Health effects

- Making people start work early is causing people to be sick, tired and **1** ....

- This is true of adults younger than **2** ....

- Not getting enough sleep has a serious effect on people's **3** ....

Changes needed

- Society needs to adapt to match people's **4** ....

- Students studying for a University degree should begin at **5** ....

- Companies that make people start work early can reduce the **6** .... of their business

- Poor sleep is an **7** .... problem that affects everyone

Questions 8–12

*Look at the following statements (**Questions 8–12**) and the list of people below.*

*Match each statement with the correct person/group of people, **A–D**.*

NB You may use any letter more than once.

8 More sleep will help students with less opportunities.

9 We cannot change our natural sleep patterns.

10 People with poor sleep will have an earlier death.

11 People who get up early do not work effectively.

12 More sleep for children could improve the whole of society.

List of people/institution
A Dr Paul Kelley
B Prof Russell Foster
C Researchers at the University of Warwick and the University of Naples Federico II
D A Department of Education spokesperson

Question 13

*Choose the correct letter, **A, B, C** or **D**.*

How can we improve our sleep?

A Reduce our levels of melatonin.

B Allow natural light into the room.

C Create a sleep routine.

D Set an alarm clock to get up.

Vocabulary 2: Collocations

Wordlist on page 214 of the Student's Book.

1 For **1–9** below, replace the <u>underlined</u> phrase with a suitable collocation. Change the form as necessary.

Example:

There are <u>a lot of</u> benefits to cutting staff costs. (enjoy/derive/considerable/accrue)
There are considerable benefits to cutting staff costs.

1 The advantages <u>are more significant than</u> the disadvantages. (take/huge/gain/outweigh)

2 He <u>threw away</u> the opportunity of a brilliant career. (boost/once in a lifetime/seize/waste)

3 Success <u>is related to</u> hard work. (achieve/enormous/depends on/guarantee)

4 She has excellent <u>job</u> prospects in this position. (offer/total/boost/career)

5 There is a <u>clear</u> disadvantage in leaving school early. (have/suffer/distinct/obvious)

6 The project was a <u>complete</u> failure. (result in/total/ensure/enjoy)

7 His CV shows <u>little in the way of</u> achievement. (outstanding/represent/a lack of/impressive)

8 There <u>could be</u> improvement in her work. (huge/make/show/room for)

9 She <u>should be given</u> a chance. (deserve/good/arise/throw away)

2 Match phrases **1–8** to collocations **a–h**.

1 improve your chances

2 a chance unlikely to ever happen again

3 lead to something not being achieved

4 to lose an opportunity

5 the chance for things to get better

6 how well something does is connected to something else

7 something that is clearly negative

8 something someone has done well

a once in a lifetime opportunity

b success depends on

c boost your prospects

d distinct disadvantage

e result in failure

f outstanding achievement

g room for improvement

h throw away a chance

3 Complete the sentences **1–4** with four of the collocations from exercise 2.

1 I have a _____ to travel the world for a year.

2 I think you need to get some more work experience to _____ of getting a permanent job.

3 What _____ are you most proud of?

4 Your work is good but there's definitely _____ .

1.7 **SECTION 3** *Questions 21–30*

Questions 21–25

*Choose **FIVE** letters, **A–H**.*

Which of these **FIVE** factors affecting happiness does Sue say
Richard Layard mentions in his book *Happiness*?

A Money   **E** Holidays

B Health   **F** Values

C Housing   **G** Freedom

D Relationships   **H** Free time

Questions 26–28

Complete the sentences below.

*Write **NO MORE THAN ONE WORD AND/OR A NUMBER** for each answer.*

26 Being part of a strong society could possibly make people .... longer.

27 There are .... key things that determine how happy a country is.

28 When a person's salary drops by a .... their happiness is hardly affected.

Questions 29 and 30

Answer the questions below.

*Write **ONE WORD ONLY** for each answer.*

29 What is the most important thing to feel happy in your work? ....

30 What's the most important thing about friendship and community? ....

Language focus: Conditionals 1

(G) Grammar reference on page 223 of the Student's Book.

1 Choose the correct tense to complete these sentences.

1 first conditional

If I (leave/left) now, I ('ll catch/would catch) the train.

2 second conditional

If I (tried/had tried) harder, I (would get/would have got) better results.

3 third conditional

If I (had prepared/prepare) more, I (would have got/will get) the job.

2 Match **A–C** to the main uses **1–3** below.

A first conditional

B second conditional

C third conditional

1 To talk about things in the past happening differently from the way they happened – often to express regret.

2 To talk about something unreal and imagined – or something we are not sure of.

3 To talk about future events we are quite sure about.

3 Use the first conditional and the word in brackets to comment on these situations.

1 Paul won't be able to get in because the office might be closed. (if)

2 I'll stay in the job. But I want more money. (unless)

3 She needs to leave now or she might not get her train. (otherwise)

4 We might lose the contract. If we do, Harry will be upset. (if)

4 What does the *if*-clause in each sentence **1–4** below mean? Write your answers in sentences that use *isn't, is* or *might*.

Example:

If this office was tidy, I could find things.
The office isn't tidy.

1 If we're late for the meeting, we can get a taxi.

2 I would call you if my phone was working.

3 If Hayley calls, can you tell her I'll ring back?

4 I would meet you if I wasn't so busy.

5 Comment on the situations using the third conditional.

1 I think John didn't get the job because he needed to give a better presentation.

2 He wanted to go to university but he didn't get good grades at school.

3 He didn't come to the meeting so I think he didn't know about it. Normally he comes.

4 I booked the table late so we can't go to Quattros.

Writing
Task 2

1 Look at the following Task 2 question and then answer questions **1–3** below.

> **WRITING TASK 2**
>
> You should spend about 40 minutes on this task.
>
> Write about the following topic:
>
> > *Some secondary schools provide students with a general education across a range of subjects whereas others focus on fewer subjects related to a particular career.*
> >
> > *Do you think the advantages of a focused education outweigh the disadvantages?*
>
> Give reasons for your answer and include any relevant examples from your own knowledge or experience.
>
> Write at least 250 words.

1 What is the main topic you need to cover?

2 What two specific angles do you need to cover?

3 Do you need to give your own opinion?

2 Look at the model answer in exercise 3 and decide which is the correct outline below, **A** or **B**.

> **Outline A**
>
> 1 introduction with opinion
> 2 advantages of a focused education
> 3 disadvantages of a focused education
> 4 disadvantages of a focused education
> 5 conclusion

> **Outline B**
>
> 1 introduction with opinion
> 2 advantages and disadvantages of a focused education
> 3 advantages of a focused education
> 4 disadvantages of a focused education
> 5 conclusion

3 Look at paragraph C in the model answer below and find features **1–5**. Sometimes more than one answer is possible.

1 the results

2 a topic sentence

3 an explanation/opinion

4 a disadvantage

5 an adjective of evaluation

> **A** School education has a significant impact on people's future chances in life and the focus on specific subjects can enhance or hinder these opportunities. While there are some advantages to a specific education, I feel that the drawbacks outweigh the advantages of a general education.
>
> **B** The main benefit of focusing on a smaller range of subjects related to one particular career is that the individual will be better prepared to start working life. Some people argue that they will have a deeper knowledge of the key skills required to undertake the tasks in their work. Furthermore, many argue that a number of subjects studied in school are not useful in future working life.
>
> **C** It is debatable whether we should focus on a wider or narrower range of subjects. I feel that focusing on a narrow range of subjects when young is detrimental. The lack of diversity could actually hinder someone's life chances. At such a young age very few people know what their strengths are and what career they want to spend the rest of their life working in. By not studying certain subjects the opportunities available could be severely limited.
>
> **D** Furthermore, if a student goes to a technical secondary school and leaves behind foreign languages, for example, they will face significant challenges if they need to take a language up in the future. Careers change frequently and individuals may be held back from their career path.
>
> **E** In conclusion, there are both advantages and disadvantages involved in having a focused education, but in my opinion the benefits of a general education outweigh the disadvantages.

4 Find words in paragraph C in the model answer that mean:

1 very negative

2 not enough

3 to limit

5 We usually present the opposing view to our own in the first paragraph after the introduction. Why do you think we do this?

6 Now write your own answer to the task.

Vocabulary: Nouns relating to places

Wordlist on page 215 of the Student's Book.

1 For **1–8** below, <u>underline</u> the correct noun in *italics*.

1 The national park is considered a real beauty *spot/space/district*.

2 The business *district/location/neighbourhood* is to the south of the city.

3 The city is well-known for its green *location/region/space*.

4 Barcelona is one of my favourite *neighbourhoods/settings/places* to visit.

5 Our offices are in an amazing *location/place/region* right next to the Thames.

6 There are lots of shops and services in the *space/vicinity/spot*.

7 The *location/setting/area* close to the station is quite run down.

8 My *neighbourhood/space/vicinity* is an upcoming area where lots of people want to live.

2 Choose the phrase **a–c** you most associate with phrases **1–10**.

1 a secluded spot	**a** located near a lake	**b** stretching into the distance	**c** full of shops and cafés
2 an empty desert	**a** covered with trees	**b** located near a lake	**c** with huge sand dunes and no people
3 a wooded hillside	**a** covered with trees	**b** with huge sand dunes and no people	**c** with no houses, just open fields
4 in a beautiful setting	**a** with lots of cars and people	**b** overlooking the sea	**c** full of shops and cafés
5 an open space	**a** full of shops and cafés	**b** with lots of cars and people	**c** with no houses, just open fields
6 a noisy neighbourhood	**a** full of shops and cafés	**b** covered with trees	**c** full of wildlife
7 a sandy beach	**a** located near a lake	**b** stretching into the distance	**c** with no houses, just open fields
8 in a lively district	**a** surrounded by trees	**b** full of shops and cafés	**c** full of wildlife
9 a temperate zone	**a** full of shops and cafés	**b** with lots of cars and people	**c** full of wildlife
10 a rugged mountain	**a** with huge sand dunes and no people	**b** stretching into the distance	**c** full of wildlife

3 Put the words in *italics* into the correct order.

1 I live in a *house large overlooking open wide* fields.

2 My family home is *trees surrounded by that are all sorts of full* of wildlife.

3 My ideal place to live is in a *full of cafés shops busy city and*.

4 Our family has a holiday *located home with huge on the coast people and no dunes*.

READING PASSAGE

*You should spend about 20 minutes on **Questions 1–13**, which are based on the
Reading Passage below.*

Maps in history

Humans have been sketching maps for millennia,
but Claudius Ptolemy was the first to use math and
geometry to develop a manual for how to map the
planet using a rectangle and intersecting lines – one
that resurfaced in 13th-century Byzantium and was used
until the early 17th century. The Alexandria-based Greek
scholar, who may never have drawn a map himself,
described the latitude and longitude of more than
8,000 locations in Europe, Asia, and Africa, projecting a
north-oriented, Mediterranean-focused world that was
missing the Americas, Australasia, southern Africa, the
Far East, the Pacific Ocean, and most of the Atlantic
Ocean. Ptolemy's *Geography* was a 'book with a 1,500-
year legacy,' says Brotton, a professor of Renaissance
studies at Queen Mary University of London.

The map produced by the German cartographer Martin
Waldseemüller in 1507 is considered to be the most
expensive map in the world because, as Brotton notes,
it is 'America's birth certificate' – a distinction that
prompted the Library of Congress in Washington, USA,
where it still survives today, to buy it from a German
prince for $10 million. It is the first map to recognise the
Pacific Ocean and the separate continent of 'America',
which Waldseemüller named in honour of the then still-
living Amerigo Vespucci, who identified the Americas as
a distinct landmass. The map consists of 12 woodcuts
and incorporates many of the latest discoveries
by European explorers (you get the sense that the
woodcutter was asked at the last minute to make room
for the Cape of Good Hope). 'This is the moment when
the world goes bang, and all these discoveries are made
over a short period of time,' Brotton says.

Maps often have political undertones to them and this
is the case with the map produced by the Portuguese
cartographer Diogo Ribeiro. Ribeiro's World Map of
1529 was composed during a bitter dispute between
Spain and Portugal over the Moluccas, an island chain
in present-day Indonesia and hub for the spice trade. In
1494, the two countries had signed a treaty dividing the
world's newly discovered lands in two. After Ferdinand
Magellan's expedition circumnavigated the globe for
the first time in 1522, Ribeiro, working for the Spanish
crown, placed the 'Spice Islands', inaccurately, just
inside the Spanish half of his seemingly scientific world
map. Ribeiro may have known that the islands (which
appear on the far-left and far-right sides of the map)
actually belonged to Portugal, but he also knew who
paid the bills. 'This is the first great example of politics
manipulating geography,' Brotton says.

Beginning under Louis XIV, four generations of the
Cassini family presided over the first attempt to survey
and map every metre of a country. The Cassinis used
the science of triangulation to create a nearly 200-sheet
topographic map of France, which French revolutionaries
nationalised in the late 18th century. This, Brotton says,

'is the birth of what we understand as modern nation-
state mapping ... whereas, before, mapmaking was in
private hands. Now, in the Google era, mapmaking is
again going into private hands.'

In 1569, Mercator, the Flemish-German cartographer,
produced a map designed for European navigators.
Mercator's allegedly Eurocentric projection was a map
depicting countries and continents according to their
actual surface area – hence the smaller-than-expected
northern continents, and Africa and South America
appearing, in Brotton's words, 'like long, distended
tear drops.' In 1973, the left-wing German historian
Arno Peters unveiled an alternative to the 'equal area'
projection, which was nearly identical to an earlier
design by the Scottish clergyman James Gall and
was a hit with the press and progressive NGOs (non-
governmental organisations). But critics argued that any
projection of a spherical surface onto a plane surface
involves distortions, and that Peters had amplified these
by committing serious mathematical errors. 'No map is
any better or worse than any other map,' Brotton says.
'It's just about what agenda it pursues.'

In June 2012, Brian McClendon, an executive at
Google, wrote in a blog post that Google was engaged
in nothing less than a 'never-ending quest for the
perfect map'. 'We've been building a comprehensive
base map of the entire globe – based on public and
commercial data, imagery from every level (satellite,
aerial and street level) and the collective knowledge of
our millions of users,' McClendon noted. By strapping
cameras to the backs of intrepid hikers, mobilising
users to fact-check map data, and modelling the world
in 3D, he added, Google was moving one step closer
to mapmaking perfection. 'All cultures have always
believed that the map they valorise is real and true
and objective and transparent, Brotton, a professor
of Renaissance studies at Queen Mary University of
London, told me. All maps are always subjective ...
Even today's online geospatial applications on all your
mobile devices and tablets, be they produced by Google
or Apple or whoever, are still to some extent subjective
maps.' There are, in other words, no perfect maps –
just maps that (more-or-less) perfectly capture our
understanding of the world at discrete moments
in time.

Questions 1–5

*Complete each sentence with the correct ending, **A–G**, below.*

1 People originally

2 Claudius Ptolemy possibly

3 The Greek scholar's work

4 The most valuable map

5 America was named after
the person who

A didn't draw a map himself.

B didn't include the Mediterranean.

C didn't use maths to create maps.

D included the continent of America.

E is no longer in the American Library of Congress.

F mainly described the Mediterranean.

G identified it as a separate area of land.

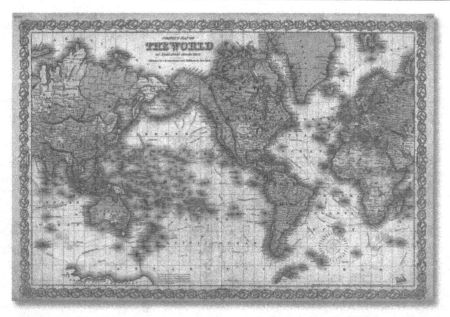

Questions 6–10

Do the following statements agree with the information in the Reading Passage?

Write:

TRUE   *if the statement agrees with the information*
FALSE   *if the statement disagrees with the information*
NOT GIVEN *if there is no information on this*

6 Diogo Ribeiro produced a non-political map.

7 Spain and Portugal controlled many newly discovered countries.

8 Spain was Portugal's main trading partner.

9 One family produced the first map of a single country.

10 Revolutionaries used the France map to nationalise the country.

Questions 11–13

Answer the questions.

*Write **ONE WORD ONLY** from the passage for each answer.*

11 When looking at Peters' map, what did critics say was caused when you take
something from a round surface to a flat one?

12 What type of mistakes had Peters made?

13 What is Google getting nearer to doing at the highest level?

Language focus: Referring in a text

G Grammar reference on page 223 of the Student's Book.

1 What does the word in **bold** refer to in **1–3** below?

1 Rural to urban migration largely happens for economic reasons. **It** often occurs during periods of industrialisation.

2 Push and pull factors are the main influences on migration. **These** are often the reason why someone leaves an area and goes to another one.

3 Managing the development of new infrastructure is the key to success. **This** will allow a city to grow in a controlled manner.

2 Complete the sentences with a pronoun from the box. Some words may be used more than once.

it	these	this	they	his	her	that	these

1 Town planners make decisions about the development of a town. _____ need to decide how best to spend the money available to improve an area.

2 Sir Norman Foster is an influential British architect. _____ work includes famous buildings such as 30 St Mary Axe (also known as the Gherkin) in London, redevelopment of the Reichstag building in Germany, and the Hearst Tower in New York. _____ are just a few examples of the work Foster and Partners have been involved in developing.

3 More than 40% of architecture graduates are women but despite _____ no more than 12% of architects are women.

4 In 2004, the Iraqi-British architect Zaha Hadid became the first woman to be awarded the Pritzker Prize. _____ is the top award given to a living architect. _____ projects include the Lois & Rosenthal Centre for Contemporary Art in Cincinnati and the BMW Central Building in Leipzig.

5 One building that has been proposed but not yet built is the X-Seed 4000 in Tokyo. If _____ tower were to be built it would be the world's tallest building and could house over a million people.

6 There are a number of features that make the Gherkin in London energy efficient. _____ features include open shafts between each floor and curved windows for increased natural light.

Hearst Tower, New York

3 Use pronouns to remove the repetition from each sentence.

1 The town was once run down but now the town has been redeveloped, modernised and expanded.

2 The standard of living in this country is rising, and the rising standard of living is set to continue.

3 I like running in the park in the evening, running in the park in the evening is much cooler and quieter than doing so in the day.

4 The government should pass laws to control urban development. Passing laws to control urban development would make it more controlled.

5 The chief architect presented her plans to the local government. The chief architect was confident of gaining the local government approval.

Listening
Section 4

🎧 2.1 **SECTION 4** *Questions 31–40*

Questions 31–40

Complete the notes below.

*Write **NO MORE THAN THREE WORDS AND/ OR A NUMBER** for each answer.*

Rural to urban migration

More than **31** .... of people in European countries live in urban areas

This is the equivalent of everyone in **32** .... moving somewhere else

China's **33** .... reduced families in the countryside to 1.5 children

The Hukou System **34** .... the number of rural to urban migrants

The limits were **35** .... because of China's major economic policy

Migrants born after 1990 have less **36** .... as they leave at age 17

An increase in income has led to health-related problems such as **37** ....

38 .... per cent of kids younger than one have a higher survival rate in urban areas

Many migrants can now afford items that improve their **39** ....

Urban residents have increased opportunity to continue in higher levels of **40** ....

Verbs relating to changes in places

1 Match verbs **1–6** to definitions **a–f**.

1 replace
2 knock down/demolish
3 turn into/convert
4 chop down
5 transform
6 was built in place of

a To destroy something, especially a building.
b To put one thing in place of another.
c To change the use of something.
d To change dramatically.
e To remove trees from an area.
f To construct as an alternative to something else.

2 Complete the sentences with the most suitable verb, **1–6**, from exercise 1 in the correct form. There may be more than one correct answer.

1 The old warehouse was _____ and new housing was built to _____ it.

2 The hotel was _____ into flats.

3 The trees were _____ to make way for the new train line.

4 The town centre has been _____ into a more modern and contemporary environment.

5 The park and ride facilities _____ a new train station.

3 Complete the sentences with the correct form of the words from the box.

expand	extend	construct	change	demolish
convert	alter	become	take place	

1 The _____ of the shopping mall has taken it from 2,000 square metres to 3,000 square metres.

2 The front of the building was _____ slightly to make it look more modern.

3 The road has been _____ along the coast.

4 The construction of a new shopping mall completely _____ the town centre.

5 The _____ of the old offices and construction of new ones took a year to complete.

6 A new school was _____ on the edge of town.

7 Residents had objected to the _____ of the old house to _____ a hotel.

8 An event to showcase the plans _____ in the town hall.

4 Correct the mistakes in the sentences.

1 They made small alters to the layout of the park.

2 The extend was completed in 2016.

3 They plan to construction a new town hall.

4 A group of hotels plans to conversion the old prison into a hotel.

Writing

Task 1

1 Read the task below. What do you have to focus on, **a** or **b**?

   a Describing each map individually.

   b How the town has changed.

WRITING TASK 1

You should spend about 20 minutes on this task.

> *The maps below show changes in the town of Hillingford between 2000 and 2015.*
> *Summarise the information by selecting and reporting the main features, and make*
> *comparisons where necessary.*

Write at least 150 words.

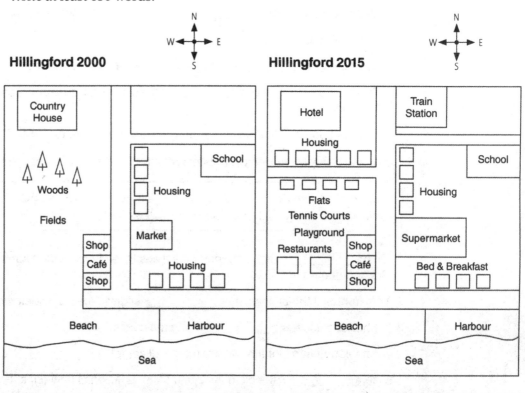

---

2 Look at the map of Hillingford in 2000. For **1–7** below, <u>underline</u> the correct phrase in *italics*.

   1 *South of/West of* the country house there are some woods.

   2 *In the east of/In the west of* the town there is a school.

   3 *In the north of/In the west of* the town there is a country house.

   4 *West of/East of* the school is some housing.

   5 The road *is/runs* halfway along the beach.

   6 The harbour *is situated/runs* next to the sea.

   7 *There is/There are* a market along the main road.

3 Now look at the map of Hillingford in 2015. Complete these sentences to describe the changes to the map.

1 The tennis courts have been built on the site of _____ .

2 The country house has become _____ .

3 The school has _____ .

4 The market has been turned into _____ .

5 The woods have been given over to _____ .

6 The housing near the harbour has been replaced by _____ .

4 Insert phrases **a–g** into the correct spaces **1–7** to complete the model answer.

a has been converted into a hotel

b have been built on the site of the fields

c the construction of a train station in the north of the town

d has now been reconstructed to become a small tourist town

e extended further west along the coast

f The woods have been chopped down to construct

g has been turned into bed and breakfast accommodation

The maps show the changes that took place in Hillingford between 2000 and 2015. The town has undergone a complete transformation and modernisation.

Originally, the town was probably a small fishing village that **1** _____ . The country house in the north west of the town **2** _____ and the housing near the harbour **3** _____ . In the west of the town, restaurants, tennis courts and a playground **4** _____ . The road has also been **5** _____ . **6** _____ further housing and flats in the north west of the town. Additionally, a road has been added to reach these new developments. This transformation of the town into a more urban area has also seen **7** _____ .

5 (Circle) the adverbs of location in the completed model answer.

6 Write your own answer to the Task 1 question.

9 What is beauty?

Vocabulary: Beauty

Wordlist on page 215 of the Student's Book.

1 Read the descriptions of the statues and monuments. Match them to the pictures.

1

The world famous moai are monolithic statues on Easter Island, one of the most isolated islands in the world. They were built in tribute to powerful leaders, but the isolation and forgotten past makes me feel melancholic.

4

I think the Egyptian pyramids are world famous. Nearby is a statue commonly known as the Sphinx. It is a stone statue of a creature with a lion's body and a human head. I think this ancient sculpture is the oldest known monument in the world.

2

The most famous statue in my country is the majestic Genghis Khan Equestrian Statue. It's just east of the capital Ulaanbaatar. The statue is 40 metres tall on the bank of the Tuul River. I think people who visit it should walk up to the head of the horse for views across the spacious countryside.

5

The statue of Mevlana Rumi (a 13th-century mystic, poet, and theologian) in Izmir, Turkey, is 20 metres in height. It's a magnificent statue and below it you can sit in a café for a relaxing drink.

3

One of the most famous statues in Singapore is the Merlion. It's a lion-headed fish from local mythology. The Merlion of Sentosa is a 37-metre-tall stone statue. In Singapore, it's our national symbol.

2 Find words in descriptions **1–5** in exercise 1 that match **a–f** below.

   a beautiful and impressive

   b big, beautiful, or impressive in a calm and serious way

   c somewhere with a lot of space

   d the hard substance rocks are made from

   e very old

   f a feeling of sadness

3 Match words **1–10** below to definitions **a–j**.

1 evoke	**a**	a height bigger than average
2 tall	**b**	to describe something you admire a lot because it is very good or large
3 thoughtful	**c**	extremely impressive
4 impressive	**d**	something that expresses an idea clearly and makes you have a strong reaction to it
5 dazzling	**e**	reminding you of the past in a positive way
6 humbling	**f**	to be affected by something, especially to make you feel sad or angry
7 ecstatic	**g**	making you realise that you are not as important, good, clever, etc. as you thought
8 emotional	**h**	to affect someone's emotions in a very powerful way
9 overwhelmed	**i**	very happy
10 nostalgic	**j**	to make you think seriously and deeply as a reaction to seeing it

4 Circle the words, **1–10**, in exercise 3 that are used to physically describe a statue or monument. Underline the words that describe how someone might feel about it.

5 Use the words from exercise 3 to write an opinion of the statues and monuments in exercise 1.

READING PASSAGE

*You should spend about 20 minutes on **Questions 1–14**, which are based on the Reading Passage below.*

The beauty of age

A Architecture is a direct and substantial representation of history and place. By preserving historic structures, we are able to share the very spaces and environments in which the generations before us lived. Historic preservation is the visual and tangible conservation of cultural identity. Architecture is one aspect of our heritage with which we can interact and adapt. Some buildings have specific historic context and must be meticulously and exactly preserved. Most buildings, however, must be lived in, interacted with and maintained by the public. These buildings change with us, thus recording a piece of each generation's story. We have an obligation to respect this community resource and preserve it for future generations. Preservation works within the established history and location of cities and towns to build on the rich culture already at hand.

Lowell National Historical Park

B In addition to solidifying a community's past, preservation can help strengthen a community's future. Historic buildings help create vibrant, cultural downtowns that draw tourism, art, festivals, and other activities which in turn draw investment, revenue, and economic growth. A dynamic historic downtown can be the centrepiece of community life: a place to shop, invest, create and live. Simultaneously, preservation can be a tool to boost the economy and quality of life. Local residents benefit through interpretive components such as learning and recreational activities that complement an historic site's didactic offerings and illustrate a special meaning between its past, present and future. The more the community is involved, the more attractive and effective an area will become for locals and visitors.

C In the past, historic preservation has been considered a luxury practice, but in recent years, research of the economic and public benefits have revealed that it is a powerful tool in sustaining local economy, creating jobs, and even generating capital. The aesthetic, cultural and historical benefits of preservation are well known, but now, communities are realising that there are positive economic effects also.

D A number of studies have been conducted throughout the United States in recent years, analysing the economic benefits of historic preservation on property values. The results, on both state and local levels, have consistently reported that properties in historic districts appreciate significantly faster than comparable properties not located in historic districts. Property value is determined by the buyers and sellers of the market and when dealing with historic properties, those buyers and sellers must recognise the significance of the historic properties in order for the value to remain high. Studies have given evidence that we, as a society, value those buildings and homes that represent our collective history. These findings make investment in historic properties economically beneficial.

E Historic districts do have aesthetic stipulations, but they are not intended to hinder property owners. Bylaws help ensure that the character of the neighbourhood remains intact. The stability provided by these standards usually raises property values because investors can be assured that the historic nature of the district will remain intact. According to Donovan D. Rypkema, a scholar from Columbia University in the field of preservation economics, local district preservation commissions can have a positive effect, 'It has been found that when a local district has the greatest positive impact on property values four variables are usually in place: clear, written design guidelines for the affected properties; staff for the preservation commission; active educational outreach by the staff and commission to property owners, real estate brokers, architects, builders, etc.; and consistent and predictable decisions by the commission.'

F Unfortunately, the international style of architecture, for all the beauty of its best work, had the damaging effect of making our cities more uniform and bland. In its debased form of concrete and glass slabs, it can be seen from Aberdeen to Plymouth, New York to Caracas and Sydney to Kuala Lumpur. Post-modernism has an equally patchy record, though contemporary buildings like the Ark in Hammersmith, looming like an ocean liner over an inner urban motorway, are encouraging. It shows that even basic amenities can be a joy to look at and use. But while the pendulum of architectural fashion has swung back towards traditional materials, local character is still under threat from the standardised corporate style of commercial interests. The chain stores, with their expensively-designed images, dominate British towns, making them look increasingly indistinguishable – and dull. People enjoy difference, variety and individuality. They love the drama of the unplanned townscape, where buildings old and new, good and not so good, tell their own long story of the town.

G There are many positive examples of developments across the world. In Baltimore, development was triggered by the city council in the late 1950s, followed by a programme of architectural competitions and the establishment of aesthetic criteria in planning to increase quality. Lowell, widely seen as the first US industrial town based on cotton and textiles, was in decline in 1970. It initiated 22 heritage projects re-furbishing warehouses to create museums, heritage and visitor centres, shops and restaurants. This was presented as an 'urban cultural park' (the Lowell National Historical Park) and is now considered to have been very successful in changing the image of Lowell, and attracting tourists. Placing arts at the centre of redevelopment may be one way to maintain beauty and uniqueness in a city.

Questions 1–7

The Reading Passage has seven paragraphs, **A–G**.

Which paragraph contains the following information?

1 Laws protecting old buildings maintain the standard of an area as a whole.

2 Building prices rise quicker in old areas.

3 Appropriate town planning creates cultural and other facilities that draw visitors.

4 Residents should help protect their own area.

5 Preserving buildings allows us to build on our cultural past.

6 Previously, local communities did not realise preserving buildings was important.

7 People prefer cities to be unique.

Questions 8–14

Do the following statements agree with the claims of the writer in the Reading Passage?
Write:

    YES   *if the statement agrees with the claims of the writer*
    NO   *if the statement disagrees with the claims of the writer*
    NOT GIVEN *if it is impossible to say what the writer thinks about this*

8 We should not change the use of old buildings.

9 Historic areas often have modern uses.

10 Communities frequently want to change old areas.

11 Keeping historic areas can be good for people's finances today.

12 Communities don't understand the benefits of preserving old buildings.

13 All modern architecture is not beautiful.

14 Beauty was a factor considered in the regeneration of Baltimore.

Word building: Prefixes *under-* and *over-*

1 Choose the best option in *italics* to complete each sentence.

1 The gallery was *over/under*rated. I didn't enjoy it at all.

2 The project was *over/under*funded. It ran out of money five years before completion.

3 Many people often *over/under*estimate the value of their own house. They usually want too much money for it.

4 She should be paid a lot more. She's definitely *over/under*paid.

5 My boss says I'm not doing very well. I'm *over/under*performing.

6 My son hasn't started school yet, so he should be able to travel for free as he is *under/over* five.

7 When the construction boom started, builders were *over/under*employed.

8 They were *over/under*prepared for the number of visitors. They couldn't cope.

9 Everyone goes in there. The building is completely *over/under*used.

10 They were very impressed. They found the events on the day completely *over/under*whelming.

2.2 SECTION 3 Questions 21–30

Questions 21–30

Write **NO MORE THAN TWO WORDS AND/OR A NUMBER** *for each answer.*

21 The tour won't be traditional. It needs to be .... tour. Not something you can find online easily.

22 The Empire State Building is so famous and it often has ....

23 The tour will begin with ....

24 The tour should mainly look at ....

25 Nassau County Museum of Art gardens are .... to visit. The gardens are very traditional but contain contemporary sculptures.

26 The museum has lots of .... by artists from the last two centuries.

27 Long Island Museum has different displays of ....

28 The main cost is for ....

29 The cost per person when full is ....

30 Another way to make money is to do business with ....

Language focus: Modal verbs for evaluating

(G) Grammar reference on page 224 of the Student's Book.

1 Rewrite the sentences using the modal verb in brackets.

Example:

They built a new motorway. I don't think it was a good idea.

They shouldn't have built a new motorway. (should build)

1 I don't know if she called.

_____ (might call).

2 This area is run down. The government needs to spend money on it.

_____ (ought to) spend money on it.

3 I think something happened. Everyone looks sad.

_____ (must happen) because everyone looks sad.

4 I don't know if he is here.

_____ (might be) here.

5 I don't think the company dealt with this very well.

_____ (could deal) with this better.

6 I haven't done as much work as I thought.

_____ (should do) more work by now.

7 I think the building is really expensive.

_____ (must be) really expensive.

2 Correct the mistakes in these sentences.

1 I shouldn't have not gone to work. I felt terrible.

2 They chopped down the trees. They should chop down the trees.

3 They should to clean up the graffiti.

4 The building must have been finished now. There are very few workers here.

5 They must finish by now. It doesn't take that long.

6 It might have been ready, but I'm not certain.

3 Which sentences in exercise 2 express the following:

a a conclusion

b a regret

c a suggestion

d a criticism

e an expectation

f a possibility

Writing
Task 2

1 Read the task below and answer questions **1** and **2** that follow.

WRITING TASK 2

You should spend about 40 minutes on this task.

Write about the following topic:

> *Some people believe that modern architecture has made cities more attractive in the last century.*
> *To what extent do you agree or disagree?*

Give reasons for your answer and include any relevant examples from your own knowledge or experience.

Write at least 250 words.

1 Do you need to give your personal opinion on the topic?

2 Does the question ask you to compare two specific things?

2 Match causes **1–8** with effects **a–h**.

1 Modern cities are compact which can lead to

2 Thanks to the number of tall buildings

3 As a result of their planning,

4 New constructions are frequently made by international firms which can have a negative effect on

5 Modern cities are generally cleaner, which in turn

6 Ancient cities make

7 Tourism to an area can be affected by

8 Some countries have spent enormous amounts of money producing

a can make them more attractive.

b more people in a small area.

c people can feel trapped and oppressed.

d people feel more connected with their community and culture.

e newer cities can feel more ordered.

f a lack of old attractive cities.

g vast but attractive modern cities.

h a city's appearance as it loses the local influence.

3 Replace the phrases in *italics* with phrases in the box.

| has a positive effect | they shouldn't have relaxed | focusing on |
| now lighten up | should be attractive | |

1 Architects are *looking at* many aspects when they design a new building.

2 Modern cities *need to be beautiful* as well as functional.

3 Leaving enough green, open spaces in a city *can lead to a good impact* on people's well-being.

4 Modern architectural designs and construction methods mean new buildings *brighten up* many former run-down inner-city areas.

5 *It wasn't a good idea to go easy* on the planning restrictions. The town now has far too many ugly, modern office blocks and not enough affordable housing.

4 Look at the model answer below and answer **a–d**.

    a Identify the author's main opinion.

    b In paragraph 1, find two examples where no linking word is used to express cause and effect.

    c In paragraph 2, find one example of a linking word that expresses cause and two that express effect.

    d In paragraph 3, find words that mean *to make new again* and *change significantly*.

Around the world, cities are constantly expanding and changing as more and more people move to urban areas. Some people feel that modern architecture is not attractive, however, I feel that when it is well planned it can significantly enhance the appearance of a city.

When the development and construction of new buildings happens in a rapid manner it can have a detrimental effect on a city's appearance. Many modern buildings are cheap to build in comparison to historic ones due to the materials and construction methods used. As a result, a building can have a simplistic or ugly design. It can also age quickly and consequently look run-down. Many modern buildings built in historic cities can also change the appearance of an area dramatically. If the surrounding area is not considered carefully it can make a once historic and attractive area much more depressing to look at.

However, modern architecture also has many positive effects. It is responsible for rejuvenating dilapidated areas of a city. Some poor and run-down parts of cities have been lightened up as a consequence of using modern architecture. Additionally, even famous old skylines can change and become even more iconic. Take London, for example, which has seen the addition of 30 St Mary Axe (otherwise known as the Gherkin) and the Shard in recent years. Both are modern yet beautiful buildings that I think have transformed London's skyline for the better.

In conclusion, while modern architecture can appear cheap and ugly, I feel it largely has a positive effect on transforming the appearance of many cities.

5 Write your own answer to the Task 2 question.

Vocabulary: Art

Wordlist on page 216 of the Student's Book.

1 Look at the list of art forms **1–7** below and cross out the word in each list **a–d** that is NOT associated with them.

1 musical	**a** artist	**b** composer	**c** singer	**d** director
2 exhibition	**a** artist	**b** editor	**c** sculptor	**d** exhibitor
3 film	**a** producer	**b** director	**c** exhibitor	**d** writer
4 book	**a** writer	**b** editor	**c** director	**d** publisher
5 video game	**a** singer	**b** programmer	**c** designer	**d** player
6 sculpture	**a** sculptor	**b** producer	**c** artist	**d** exhibitor
7 play	**a** actor	**b** director	**c** programmer	**d** designer

2 Match each sentence beginning **1–10** with an ending **a–j**.

1 She designs

2 He's an artist.

3 He has every teenager's dream job. He plays

4 He works in theatre and directed his first

5 She's performing in

6 The plots in

7 He sang several

8 Lots of people start acting

9 He composed his first

10 It took eight weeks to construct

a musical last year.

b her films are very complicated to follow.

c clothes for period drama films.

d solo songs in the musical.

e He largely draws impressionist pieces.

f video games for a living.

g the ballet *Swan Lake* this month.

h in soap operas on television.

i the art installation.

j symphony when he was a young musician of just ten.

3 Choose the correct form to complete these sentences.

1 The (exhibitor/exhibition) is open seven days a week.

2 You can meet the (sculpture/sculptor) this Friday at the exhibition.

3 The play has received a lot of (critic/criticism).

4 It's one of the most valuable (collect/collections) in the world.

5 The (scene/scenery) in the play took weeks to design and build.

6 The artist's (vision/visual) was clear for all to see.

4 Complete the text with words from the box.

plays	background	composed	highbrow
classical	critical	appreciate	abstract

He has starred in over fifty **1** _____ in the West End, but his latest one has not been received well. The theatre reviewers for the newspapers were very **2** _____ of the play and gave it poor reviews. There is a danger the play might be considered **3** _____ because people don't understand it and this prevents it appealing to a young audience.

The film is set in Rome, but much of it was filmed in the studio. The **4** _____ for the fight scene in the movie was generated by CGI, which means the special effects are amazing. Viewers are also likely to **5** _____ the excitement and tension the music creates. Perhaps not surprisingly she won an Oscar for the soundtrack, and she **6** _____ the score for his last film.

The artist wanted to create a multi-sensory experience. While walking around the gallery looking at the **7** _____ art on display, **8** _____ music is played in the background. Wind and smells of the sea are also present in the room to transport people to the coast.

READING PASSAGE

*You should spend about 20 minutes on **Questions 1–13**, which are based on the Reading Passage below.*

The Floating Piers

For sixteen days – 18 June to 3 July, 2016 – Italy's Lake Iseo was reimagined. 100,000 square metres of shimmering yellow fabric, carried by a modular floating dock system of 220,000 high-density polyethylene cubes, undulated with the movement of the waves as *The Floating Piers* rose just above the surface of the water. Visitors were able to experience this work of art by walking on it from Sulzano to Monte Isola and to the island of San Paolo, which was framed by *The Floating Piers*.

The Floating Piers was first conceived by Christo and Jeanne-Claude together in 1970. It was Christo's first large-scale project since Christo and Jeanne-Claude realised a project for Central Park, New York called *The Gates* in 2005, and since his wife, Jeanne-Claude, passed away in 2009. As with all of Christo and Jeanne-Claude's projects, *The Floating Piers* was funded entirely through the sale of Christo's original works of art.

For all of Christo and Jeanne-Claude's projects, there have been two different ways of choosing a site. In one scenario, the artists had a specific building or location in mind – such as the Pont-Neuf in Paris or the Reichstag in Berlin. In a second scenario, the artists had an idea for a project, but did not know where it would be physically located. In the case of *The Floating Piers*, Christo and Jeanne-Claude knew a floating pier would rise just above the surface of the water, but they did not know which river or lake would work best. Early renditions of what the artists envisioned were created by Christo in 1970, proposing a 2,000-metre-long inflated pier on the delta of the Río de la Plata in Argentina. It never happened because Christo and Jeanne-Claude never got a permit. Twenty-five years later, in 1995, after finishing *The Wrapped Reichstag* in Berlin, the idea of *The Floating Piers* was still running around inside the heads and hearts of the artists, so they proposed making two floating piers, 150 metres long, covered in fabric, which connected to two artificial islands in Tokyo Bay and continue on to Odaiba Park. Again, after drawings and sketches, a permit wasn't granted.

Then, in 2014, Christo remembered the lakes of northern Italy, with which he had been familiar since the 1960s when he worked and exhibited in Italy extensively. In the spring and summer of 2014, Christo and his team scouted the lakes and found Lake Iseo to be the most inspiring location for the project.

Lake Iseo is located 100 kilometres east of Milan and 200 kilometres west of Venice. 'Like all of our projects, *The Floating Piers* was absolutely free and open to the public,' says Christo. 'There were no tickets, no openings, no reservations and no owners. *The Floating Piers* was an extension of the street and belonged to everyone. Those who experienced *The Floating Piers* felt like they were walking on water – or perhaps the back of a whale. The light and water transformed the bright yellow fabric to shades of red and gold throughout the sixteen days.'

Christo paid the entire costs associated with *The Floating Piers* himself, including the permitting process, manufacturing, installation and removal of the project. He earns all of the money through the sale of his preparatory studies and early works from the 50s and 60s. He does not accept grants or sponsorships of any kind, viewing fees, donated labour (volunteer help) or money for things like posters, postcards, books, films or any other products at all. Christo firmly believes that to accept deals of this kind would alter and compromise his art. Refusing this money assures him he is working in total freedom.

A 3-kilometre-long walkway was created as *The Floating Piers* extended across the water of Lake Iseo. The piers were 16 metres wide and approximately 35 centimetres high with sloping sides. The fabric continued along 2.5 kilometres of pedestrian streets in Sulzano and Peschiera Maraglio. The piers were made of 220,000 high-density polyethylene cubes held together by over 200,000 pins. The piers were held in place by 200 anchors, each weighing 5.5 tons. These anchors were connected to the piers with 37,000 metres of rope. On top of the cubes is a layer of felt before the bright yellow fabric is placed on top.

Christo had designed *The Floating Piers* to be seen from the mountains, all around the lake, from the roads, by boat – and, of course, by walking on the piers. Neither Christo nor Jeanne-Claude flew over their previous works, because they were designed to be experienced from the ground – not from the air. Only the *Surrounded Islands* were designed to be seen also from above. This project involved surrounding eleven of the islands situated in Biscayne Bay, Greater Miami, with 6.5 million square feet (603,870 square metres) of floating pink woven polypropylene fabric. This project was designed to be experienced from the air, unlike *The Floating Piers* project, which could not be fully enjoyed from the air. Nature – the water, the wind, the sun – all of this was part of *The Floating Piers* project.

Questions 1–9

*Complete the summary using the list of words, **A–Q**, below.*

The Floating Piers project

The Floating Piers connected three main points. It also **1** .... the Island of San Paolo. It was Christo's first major project since his partner **2** .... For some of the first projects they collaborated on, they had a particular **3** .... or place they wanted to use. For other projects, they had an idea but did not know where to **4** .... it. They first wanted to place *The Floating Piers* in Argentina or Tokyo but they weren't given **5** .... Lake Iseo was chosen because it was the most **6** .... site. You did not have to **7** .... to visit the site. The project was **8** .... by Christo himself. By accepting no money, he feels **9** .... to express his art how he wants.

A died	**J** use
B funded	**K** access
C structure	**L** impressive
D fees	**M** pay
E on	**N** base
F surrounded	**O** expensive
G retired	**P** want
H person	**Q** free
I permission	

Questions 10–12

Label the diagram below.

*Write **NO MORE THAN TWO WORDS** from the passage for each answer.*

A cube from *The Floating Piers*

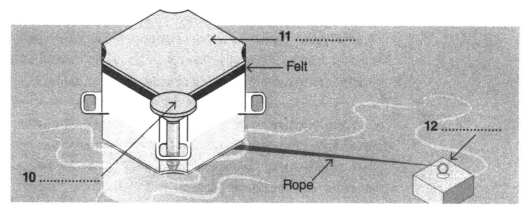

Question 13

*Answer the question. Write **NO MORE THAN TWO WORDS** from the passage.*

Where could people see *The Floating Piers* from a high position, but not by flying over it?

Language focus: Defining and non-defining relative clauses

(G) Grammar reference on page 224 of the Student's Book.

1 Read texts **A** and **B**. Identify the defining and non-defining clauses.

A

Lisa: Hamish Lightfoot has written an autobiography.

Tommy: Who?

Lisa: You know. The film star who played the hero in *Majestic*.

Tommy: I don't think I've seen that.

Lisa: You have. It's the film that we watched together online.

Tommy: Oh, the one with the car explosion at the end that killed his girlfriend?

Lisa: No, you're getting confused. He plays a man whose sister is really successful and he has achieved nothing.

Tommy: Oh yes, I remember. So he's written an autobiography? But he's only 25! That's amazing!

B

Hamish Lightfoot, who has starred in films such as *Majestic* and *Flying by Morning*, has written his first autobiography. The 25-year-old actor has been acting since the age of five, and has appeared in over 30 films. His most famous role to date was as the young pilot in *Flying by Morning*, which won a number of awards. Fellow actor Theo Brennan said, 'There are very few actors who can be both popular and critically successful. Films which make money but also change the acting world are rare. Hamish manages to achieve both.' The book, which will be available from this Friday, costs £8.99.

---

2 Read the article below. Are clauses **1–8** defining or non-defining?

The play [1] that the students put on at the end of term was Shakespeare's *Romeo and Juliet*, [2] which was written in about 1595. The university theatre, [3] which holds about 300 people, was sold out on Friday and Saturday night. The tickets, [4] which cost twenty-five pounds, sold out in 24 hours. Harry Thomas, [5] who played Romeo, was brilliant. Unfortunately, the actress [6] who played Juliet forgot her lines on more than one occasion. The set and prop design also let down the play. Buildings [7] whose features would not look out of place on a modern high street and clothes [8] that looked like they were borrowed from another play really let the play down.

---

1 *Defining*   2 _____   3 _____   4 _____

5 _____   6 _____   7 _____   8 _____

3 For **1–6** below, <u>underline</u> the correct relative pronoun in *italics*. More than one answer might be possible.

1 The bestselling video game of all time, *which/that/who* has sold around 500 million copies, is *Tetris*.

2 Dancers *who/that/where* pass the audition and interview are able to join the Royal Ballet School.

3 Theatres *which/who/where* are not profitable are often closed down and converted into a building with a different use.

4 George R.R. Martin, *who/that/whose* fantasy books were made into the HBO series *Game of Thrones*, had to finish the books after the TV series was complete.

5 Leonardo DiCaprio, *who/whose/which* won an Oscar for the film *The Revenant* in 2016, became famous in the 1997 film *Titanic*.

6 Edvard Munch's painting *The Scream*, *which/who/that* was stolen along with *Madonna* from the Munch Museum, was recovered two years later.

Listening
Section 2

 2.3 **SECTION 2** *Questions 11–20*

Questions 11–15

Complete the flow-chart below using **NO MORE THAN TWO WORDS** *for each answer.*

College play production schedule

Choose **11** .... by Friday

↓

Choose **12** ....

↓

Appoint key casting and production staff

↓

Choose **13** ....

↓

Design and build the sets

↓

Design and create **14** ....

↓

Set up **15** ....

Questions 16–20

Complete the sentences below.

Write **NO MORE THAN TWO WORDS AND/OR A NUMBER** *for each answer.*

16 .... will take place in late March.

17 The .... will create the scenery.

18 The .... will make the outfits.

19 The show will run for ....

20 Tickets will go on sale ....

Writing
Task 2

1 Read the Task 2 question and answer questions **1** and **2** that follow.

WRITING TASK 2

You should spend about 40 minutes on this task.

Write about the following topic:

> *The number of people studying <u>art, languages and creative writing</u> often falls during difficult economic times.*
> *What do you think are the effects of this trend?*

Give reasons for your answer and include any relevant examples from your own knowledge or experience.

Write at least 250 words.

---

1 Do you have to talk about both positive and negative effects?

2 How could you summarise the subjects <u>underlined</u> above in one or two words?

2 Look at the student's essay plan below. Is this student going to focus on:

a positive effects only?

b negative effects only?

c both positive and negative effects?

Student's essay plan

Paragraph 1 A decrease in creative output
Paragraph 2 Job shortages in more popular areas
Paragraph 3 Narrower set of skills across society

---

3 Which introduction matches the plan in exercise 2?

Introduction 1

A fall in the arts subjects during financially challenging periods is perhaps unsurprising as people become more focused on the economic benefits of their chosen course. I believe the effects of this change will be largely negative.

Introduction 2

Falling numbers in arts related subjects is clearly connected to the jobs people hope to obtain after studying. However, there are both positives and negatives for the whole of society when these choices are made.

4 Read the model answer below and find:

1 three effects

2 the results of these effects

3 examples of defining relative clauses if they exist

4 examples of non-defining relative clauses if they exist

5 an example of purpose

6 an example

7 an opinion

A fall in the arts subjects during financially challenging periods is perhaps unsurprising as people become more focused on the economic benefits of their chosen course. I believe the effects of this change will be largely negative.

The first effect could be a decrease in creative output across the country. The creative arts, which are an important part of a society, not only enrich people's lives but they also bring in income for a country. Potentially, a country could see a fall in the literature it produces, the works of art it creates, and its use of languages. For instance, fewer people learning languages may affect trade with other countries.

Not only will the creative industries be affected but so too will the wider economy. If people study a narrower range of academic subjects there is the likelihood that there will be a surplus of qualified people in these areas. Jobs which are oversubscribed will either see a fall in the salaries of these individuals or an increase in unemployment.

Lastly, across the country there will be a narrower set of skills available to society. It's important that society has people with a range of skills in order to ensure it is diverse. Skills that are in short supply will become more expensive for companies to obtain. They may even limit the range of businesses available in a country and ultimately could lead to a less diverse society.

In conclusion, falling numbers of students in the arts is likely to have a range of negative effects on the whole of society. It could lead to a less creative society, a less skilled society and even a rise in unemployment levels.

5 Write your own answer to the Task 2 question.

Vocabulary: The family

Wordlist on page 216 of the Student's Book.

1 Use the clues to complete the sentences below and the crossword.

Across

2 My husband died a long time ago. I've been a _____ for five years.

5 My _____ are from York, but my great-grandfather moved to London in 1905. We don't have any immediate family there now.

7 Most of my _____ live in the same village. My aunts, uncles, cousins and grandparents are all still in the same place.

8 My parents' parents are my _____ .

9 My mother and my father are my _____ .

Down

1 I have a _____ and two sisters.

3 My _____ is quite small. I don't know anyone beyond my great-grandparents. (6,4)

4 There are six people in our _____ – my parents, my sister and my grandparents.

6 I have two _____ – a brother and a sister.

2 Use some of the words in exercise 1 to complete the conversation.

A: Look, here's my **1** _____ .

B: How did you find out all that information about your **2** _____? I only know about my **3** _____ who are alive. I don't know anything about those who have died.

A: A lot of the information came from my **4** _____ . My dad said I should speak to them while they are still alive.

READING PASSAGE

*You should spend about 20 minutes on **Questions 1–13**, which are based on the Reading Passage below.*

The return of the multi-generational family household

A The multi-generational American family household is staging a comeback – driven, in part, by the job losses of recent years but more so by demographic changes that have been gathering steam for decades. As of 2012, a record 57 million Americans, or 18.1% of the total U.S. population, lived in a family household that contained at least two adult generations or a grandparent and at least one other generation, according to a Pew Research Center analysis of census data. This represents a significant trend reversal. Starting right after World War II, the extended family household fell out of favour with the American public. In 1940, about a quarter of the population lived in one; by 1980, just 12% did. Since bottoming out around 1980, however, the multi-generational family household has mounted a comeback. The reversal has taken place among all major demographic groups, and it appears to be the result of a mix of social and economic forces.

B One is the change in the median age of first marriage. The typical man now marries for the first time at age 28 and the typical woman at age 26. For both genders, this is about five years older than it was in 1970. One by-product of this cultural shift is that there are more unmarried 20-somethings in the population, many of whom consider their childhood home to be an attractive living situation, especially when a bad economy makes it difficult for them to find jobs or launch careers. The move into multi-generational family households has accelerated during the Great Recession that began at the end of 2007.

C Older adults were once by far the likeliest of any age group to live in a multi-generational family household. Back in 1900, fully 57% of adults aged 65 and older did so. But over the course of the 20th century, older adults grew steadily healthier and more prosperous as a result of a range of factors, including the enactment of social safety net programs such as Social Security (financial support for poor families) and improvements in medical care. With these changes came what amounted to a new intergenerational social contract within most families – namely, that older adults who had the health and resources to live independently should do so. By 1980 and 1990, just 17% of those aged 65 and older lived in a multi-generational family household. Since then, however, the trend has reversed course and the share has risen slightly – to 20%.

D One possible explanation for the recent trend reversal is an increase in what demographers refer to as 'kin availability'. The outsized Baby Boom generation is now passing through late middle age. Compared with earlier generations, it offers its elderly parents about 50% more grown children with whom they can share a household if and when their life circumstances (such as widowhood, declining health or poverty) take them in that direction. Another possible explanation is that cuts to Medicare (government health insurance for people over 65) enacted in 1997 have increased the financial incentives for those who are elderly and infirm to move in with a grown child who is able to take on the role of informal caregiver.

E Older adults are not the age group most responsible for the overall trend reversal since 1980. That distinction belongs instead to young adults – especially those aged 25 to 34. In 1980, just 11% of adults in this age group lived in a multi-generational family household. By 2012, 23.6% did. The increase in the share of young adults living with their parents is notable for another reason: its gender profile. The 25–34 age group is the only one in which significantly more men than women are living in a multi-generational family household. Among older age groups, this living arrangement is much more common among women than men. At the later stages of the life cycle, this disparity is partly explained by the fact that women are more likely than men to outlive a spouse, at which point they become more likely candidates to live with a grown child.

F The multi-generational household isn't the only growth sector in the national landscape of living arrangements. There's also been a steady long-term rise over the past century in the polar opposite kind of household – the one made up of just a single person. In 1900, just 1.1% of Americans lived in such a household. By 2012, that share had risen to 27.4%. According to a Pew Research Center survey, adults aged 65 and older who live alone report they are not in as good health and are more likely to feel sad, depressed or lonely than are older adults who live with another person (be it a spouse or some other family member). Also, a separate Pew Research survey taken in 2014 found that 40% of 18–29 year olds consider it a 'family responsibility' for adult children to take care of the elderly. However, only 19% of people aged over 65 felt that this was the case.

Questions 1–4

Complete the sentences below.

*Choose **NO MORE THAN THREE WORDS AND/OR A NUMBER** from the passage for each answer.*

1 An increase in .... and changes in the population structure are increasing multi-generational families.

2 At the end of .... more and more people stopped living in multi-generational families.

3 The change is happening because of .... and financial pressures.

4 People now .... about 5 years later.

Questions 5–8

The Reading Passage has six paragraphs, **A–F**.

Which paragraph contains the following information?

NB You may use any letter more than once.

5 It's often economically beneficial to live with your extended family.

6 As older generations became better off they wanted to live alone.

7 Older people living alone do not feel as positive.

8 The patterns for men and women moving home are different.

Questions 9–13

*Choose **FIVE** letters, **A–H**.*

Which **FIVE** of the following statements are true about multi-generational families?

A Rich people do not like to live in multi-generational families.

B The trend rapidly increased in 2007.

C Older adults in multi-generational homes tend to live longer.

D Traditionally older people usually lived in multi-generational homes.

E In older age groups, women are more likely to live in a multi-generational family.

F Multi-generational households are not the only type of household increasing.

G Young people would prefer not to live in multi-generational families.

H In 2014, old people generally didn't feel their family should look after them.

Word building: Suffixes -hood and -ship

1   Match the suffixes in sentences **1–5** below to the correct meanings, **a–e**,
    they express.

    1 They won the championship.

    2 There has been an increase in crime in the neighbourhood.

    3 My favourite part of my childhood was when I was 11 or 12 years old.

    4 You can see the standard of craftsmanship in his work.

    5 The leadership of the country changes every five years.

    a a period of time

    b a group

    c a skill

    d a state

    e an office or position

2   Add the words to the table.

relation	apprentice	~~boy~~	brother	adult	champion	partner
father	friend	musician	sister	scholar	girl	workman

-hood	-ship
boyhood	

3   Complete the sentences below with some of the words from exercise 2.

    1 I don't have a strong _____ with my parents and my brother. We've never got on
    very well.

    2 I am in _____ with a friend of mine. We run an online business together.

    3 The hardest part about _____ is all of the responsibilities – buying a house, having
    children – it's not easy!

    4 She has started an _____ in a company. She'll be fully qualified after two years.

    5 When you buy a brand-new house, you expect it to be finished to a high standard
    of _____ .

4   Match the sentences in exercise 3 to the meanings **a–e** in exercise 1.

5   Replace the phrases in *italics* with words from the box.

leadership	craftsmanship	ownership	parenthood

    1 You can see the *skill and quality* needed to produce work of this standard.

    2 The early days of *being responsible for young children* can be very tiring for both the
    mother and father.

    3 *Having the financial responsibility* of your business can be stressful, but many people
    want to become their own boss.

    4 I enjoy *being in charge of a team*. I feel I can influence people and support them in
    their role.

Listening
Section 1

2.4 **SECTION 1** *Questions 1–10*

Questions 1–6

Label the map below.

*Write the correct letter, **A–F**, next to Questions 1–6.*

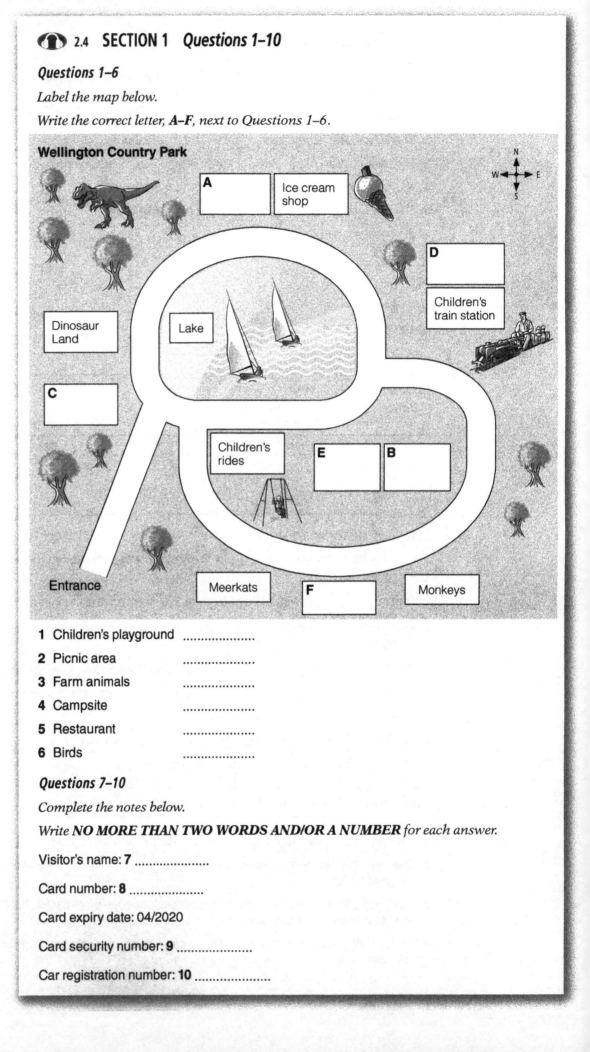

1 Children's playground ....

2 Picnic area ....

3 Farm animals ....

4 Campsite ....

5 Restaurant ....

6 Birds ....

Questions 7–10

Complete the notes below.

*Write **NO MORE THAN TWO WORDS AND/OR A NUMBER** for each answer.*

Visitor's name: **7** ....

Card number: **8** ....

Card expiry date: 04/2020

Card security number: **9** ....

Car registration number: **10** ....

Language focus: Conditionals 2

G Grammar reference on page 225 of the Student's Book.

1 Correct the mistakes.

   1 Provided that you gave children clear rules, they will behave well.

   2 As long as there aren't many problems, we would finish the work on schedule.

   3 I won't be able to come out unless I had got a babysitter.

   4 Show them how to do it. Otherwise, they would make mistakes.

   5 Supposing they had fail their exams, what will they do?

   6 Even though they would gave us two weeks for the project, I still didn't finish it.

2 (Circle) the correct conditional in *italics* to complete sentences **1–9** below.

It is possible to live a life without technology **1** *as long as/unless* you are willing to make some basic changes. It is easy to live without social media **2** *otherwise/provided that* you are willing to try. Televisions are also easy to live without **3** *unless/supposing* you need them for work. **4** *Even though/Supposing* mobile phones seem integral to our lives, most tasks we use them for are not actually necessary. **5** *Supposing/Unless* you gave up all technology for a year. What would happen to your family?

The Millars in Canada did just that. When their sons were always playing on their phones and tablets they decided they needed to make a change **6** *otherwise/if* they would not have a good family relationship. They didn't give up technology completely as they still needed some to do their jobs. So they chose to use technology only **7** *if/unless* it came from before 1986. **8** *If possible/If only*, they would spend a year living like it was in the 1980s. The result? Their work was harder and so were their daily lives, but they became much closer as a family. **9** *If only/Unless* all families could live a simpler, technology-free lifestyle perhaps society would be happier.

3 Complete the sentences using words from the box.

if ... not for	provided that	if ... would
unless	even though	supposing

   1 _____ it were _____ families taking children back in after college, many could not afford a place to live.

   2 _____ families reconnect, older people will become increasingly isolated.

   3 _____ the government spent a lot of money regenerating the area, there are still a lot of social problems, particularly crime.

   4 _____ the government invests in healthcare for the elderly, there won't be a problem.

   5 _____ the government tax increases, will people's living conditions and quality of life improve?

   6 _____ schools _____ provide free lunches for children, this could improve many children's diets.

1 Read the following Task 2 question and then answer questions **1–3** below.

WRITING TASK 2

You should spend about 40 minutes on this task.

Write about the following topic:

> *Technology has largely had a negative impact on family life.*
> *To what extent do you agree or disagree?*

Give reasons for your answer and include any relevant examples from your own knowledge or experience.

Write at least 250 words.

1 What is the main topic you need to cover?

2 Do you need to give your own opinion?

3 How long do you have to complete this task?

2 Read the model answer below and answer questions **1** and **2**.

A Technology influences nearly every aspect of family life. Hardly anything is done today the way it was fifty or sixty years ago. From cooking dinner to reading stories to children, nearly everything happens in a different way. These changes have had some negative impacts on families but largely speaking the influence has been positive.

B Some people feel that technology has had a negative effect on family life, in particular on how it has changed the way we communicate. Young children spend more and more time on phones and online and this can lead to a lack of interaction with parents. Furthermore, it has increased inactivity and, as a result, there are rising numbers of obese children.

C However, while this is true to a certain extent, I feel the positives outweigh the negatives. Many technological inventions actually save people time when used appropriately. Tasks such as banking and supermarket shopping used to require physical trips across town whereas nowadays all of this can be done on your phone in a few minutes thus leaving more time for families to spend together. In addition, technology has actually reduced the number of physical goods a family needs. DVDs, CDs and books no longer need to take up a lot of space as they can simply be stored on a laptop or tablet. Lastly, computers and the internet have made it possible for some people to work from home, meaning that they can spend more time with their family rather than commuting.

D In conclusion, while there are inevitably some negative influences that technology has had on family life, I feel these are outweighed by the positives.

1 Which sentence in the model answer introduction indicates the author's main opinion?

2 Which paragraph supports the author's point of view and which presents alternative arguments?

3 <u>Underline</u> the linking words used in the model answer and then put them in the correct column in the table below.

Provides extra information	Provides contrasting information	Cause and effect
		lead to

4 Complete each sentence **1–6** with a linker from the completed table in exercise 3. Sometimes more than one answer is possible.

1 _____ of increased working hours, parenthood has become more challenging.

2 The introduction of higher membership fees can _____ lower numbers joining the club.

3 Roles used to be clearly defined between motherhood and fatherhood. _____ nowadays there is not such a clear distinction.

4 _____ to the environmental problems caused by cars, they have also led to families living further apart from each other.

5 People who use social media a lot often do not feel positive about themselves. _____ when they reduce their usage their levels of happiness increase.

6 Mobile telephones have enabled people to stay in touch more easily. _____ , they have reduced the need for travel.

5 Which sentences in the model answer in exercise 2 could sentences **1–4** below replace?

1 If children spent less time using their electronic devices, then the increased levels of obesity might not have occurred.

2 Providing that a person's job is primarily done using a computer, it may be possible to work from home. If this occurred, there could be more time available to spend together as a family.

3 If children spent less time on phones and online, there might be increased interaction within families.

4 If music and films are stored electronically, this will enable families to have fewer physical goods filling their homes.

6 Now write your own answer to the task.

7 Check your essay. Think about:

a Is the main argument clear?

b Does each paragraph have a clear focus?

c Are clear and relevant examples provided?

d Are ideas correctly linked?

e Is the conclusion logical?

Vocabulary: Adjectives with multiple meanings

Wordlist on page 216 of the Student's Book.

1 For questions **1–7**, replace the <u>underlined</u> words in **a** and **b** with the words and phrases given in *italics*.

1 *unfamiliar   odd*

   a Have you tried Thai food? The first time I tried it, lots of the tastes were <u>strange</u> but now I love it.

   b This food tastes <u>strange</u>. I think it might be off. Can you check the date on it?

2 *recently arrived   inexperienced*

   a Let me introduce you to Michael. He's <u>new</u> in this company. He's just started in the marketing department.

   b The company are <u>new</u> in this area of business. They have more experience in engineering than design.

3 *from another country   unfamiliar*

   a I really like <u>foreign</u> food, especially spicy food from Asia.

   b It took me a long time to explain it to him because the concept was completely <u>foreign</u> to him.

4 *unusual   irregular*

   a Each vase is <u>odd</u> in shape which makes them collector's items and therefore quite valuable.

   b He's an <u>odd</u> person. Some people find him quite difficult to get along with, but I quite like him.

5 *recently made   new and different*

   a Sales have been falling for two years now. This business is in need of some <u>fresh</u> ideas.

   b When I was on holiday in Italy, we bought some delicious <u>fresh</u> bread every morning.

6 *only happens in one place   unlike anything else*

   a The island has a really diverse range of plants and animals, thanks in part to its weather system that <u>is unique to this region</u>.

   b I don't think there is much competition on the market for this. It's <u>a unique product</u> so I'm sure it will sell well.

7 *new and untouched   clean*

   a I've never used this so I'm going to sell it on eBay and say that it is <u>in pristine condition</u>.

   b My parents are visiting this weekend so I want to make the place <u>pristine</u>.

2 Change the words from exercise 1 above to suit the meaning of the dialogues. You may have to change the form of the word or replace it with a more suitable word.

1

A: What's your sister like? Is she similar to you?

B: No, she's much more unusual. She likes travelling to lots of new places, trying out new things and meeting new people.

2

A: Why are you so interested in going to Chile?

B: The country is famous for the unique of its landscape. It's such a long narrow country that you can really feel like you've been to lots of different countries.

3

A: This place is odd, but I feel like I have been here before.

B: I know what you mean. I think it's because it looks similar to Singapore.

4

A: What's the strangeness food you've ever tasted?

B: I went to London on holiday last year and we found a really unusual restaurant. I ate insects there!

5

A: What did you enjoy about travelling around India?

B: I think it was the diverse of people, food and culture. Every area is quite unique.

6

A: I'm taking my younger brother travelling this summer.

B: Has he travelled much before?

A: No, he's fresh to foreign travel.

Listening
Section 2

 2.5 **SECTION 2**   *Questions 11–20*

Questions 11–15

*Match the trip, **A–C**, to the information **11–15**.*

A Mount Etna

B Agrigento

C Caltagirone

11 Explore ancient buildings.

12 This trip is good for buying presents.

13 Taste local dishes during the day.

14 Can be shown around by a guide.

15 This is a trip for the entire day.

Cable car at Mount Etna

Questions 16–20

Complete the notes in the table below.

Write **NO MORE THAN THREE WORDS AND/OR A NUMBER** *for each answer.*

Location	Activities	Time	Price
Taormina	Visit **16** .... Visit the beach Shop and eat lunch	**17**	50 euros
Palermo	Visit various **18** .... Shopping Lunch	All day Thursday	**19** ....
Castel di Tusa	Stay in an **20**	Saturday night	150 euros

Word building: Words related to memory

1 Match the definitions **1–5** to the words **a–e**.

1 a written record of your memories

2 to learn something well enough that it is in your long-term memory

3 a monument or something else physical to remember people who died

4 things that people collect related to one thing such as a football club or a band

5 something you buy to remind you of a place or experience

a memorabilia

b memoir

c memorise

d memento

e memorial

2 For **1–9** below, <u>underline</u> the correct word in *italics*. Then decide the form of the word you have chosen, writing either **A** (adjective), **N** (noun), or **V** (verb).

1 Although he lives in Hong Kong, he collects *memorabilia/memories* connected to Manchester United FC. One day, he hopes to visit their football ground. _____

2 It is difficult to *remember/memorise* the time I spent at school in the south of France. _____

3 The test requires people to *memorise/memories* a lot of rules about driving overseas. _____

4 The former prime minister plans to publish his *memorabilia/memoir* next spring. I'm really interested to hear about his time as a child living in lots of different countries. _____

5 It's one of the most *memorable/memory* films of the last decade. It was filmed on the beautiful island of Mauritius. _____

6 I've bought some small *memoirs/mementos* to remember the place where we had such a happy vacation. _____

7 While I was in New York City, I saw some amazing sights. The Strawberry Fields *memory/memorial* is a beautiful tribute to John Lennon. _____

8 My *memory/memorise* isn't as good as it used to be. I can't remember most of the countries I've travelled to around the world. I think I've been to Lisbon, but I'm just not sure. _____

9 Could you send a *memoir/memo* to the travel team asking them to book me on a flight to Paris as soon as possible? _____

READING PASSAGE

*You should spend about 20 minutes on **Questions 1–14**, which are based on the Reading Passage below.*

The Galapagos Islands

A The Galapagos Islands are located on the Nazca tectonic plate. This perpetually moving plate is heading eastward over the Galapagos Islands hot spot, a volcanic hot spot in the east Pacific Ocean responsible for the creation of the Galapagos Islands. The islands were formed through the layering and lifting of repeated volcanic action. This geographic movement is correlated to the age of the islands, as the eastern islands (San Cristóbal and Española) are millions of years older than the western islands (Isabela and Fernandina).

B Most of the islands have a distinctive conical shape that is often associated with volcanic action. The mountainous islands have been formed through continuing volcanic eruption, building layer upon layer. Due to this volcanic formation, the islands are characterised by many steep slopes, with heights ranging from a few metres above sea level to more than 5,000 feet above sea level. Each major island, with the exception of the largest island, Isabela, consists of a single large volcano. Isabela was formed when six volcanoes joined above sea level. Geologically, the Galapagos Islands are quite young, probably no more than five million years old, compared to say the islands of Hawaii, which are more than 70 million years old. Some of the westernmost islands, which are the most volcanically active, may only be hundreds of thousands of years old and are still being formed today. The most recent eruption, after 30 years, was in 2015 from the main island of Isabela's Wolf volcano.

C Biologists are fascinated by island ecosystems and the unique species that inhabit them. For this reason, the Galapagos Islands are quite arguably the most studied archipelago in the world. The Galapagos Islands also have a unique set of environmental conditions that set them apart from all other island groups in the world. Their sunny equatorial position on the globe combined with their location amid the cool Humboldt and Cromwell ocean currents allow these special islands to display a strange mix of both tropical and temperate environments, which is reflected in the complex and unusual plants and animals that inhabit them.

D Five to ten million years ago, the tops of underwater Galapagos volcanoes appeared above water for the first time, about 600 km from mainland Ecuador in the middle of the Pacific Ocean. Those volcanic peaks were completely devoid of plant and animal life. All plants and animals that are now native to the islands must have arrived to the islands originally through some form of long-distance dispersal. When considering the diversity of species that inhabit the Galapagos Islands, it is important to note how 'unbalanced', in comparison to continental species diversity, the variety of Galapagos species are. For instance, there are many native reptile species such as turtles and iguanas, but no amphibians; there is an abundance of land and sea bird species, such as the Galapagos penguin, flightless Cormorant and waved Albatross, but very few mammals. When considering plants, those with large flowers and big seeds are absent while grasses and ferns abound.

E One theory is that the ancestors of the present-day Galapagos animals (sea lions, sea turtles, penguins) actually swam their way to the islands with the help of some swift ocean currents. On the other hand, biologists have some theories as to how the ancestors of the present-day Galapagos animals arrived on the island. One theory is reptiles and small mammals (rice rats) were carried to the islands from the South or Central American mainland on natural rafts of vegetation. The vast majority of such rafts would have sunk well before they ever reached Galapagos, but it would have only taken a handful of successful rafts to wash ashore to explain the present reptile diversity in Galapagos. This 'raft' theory of arrival also explains why there are no native amphibians, few mammals, and many reptiles in the Galapagos Islands – reptiles are the best adapted to deal with the harsh salty and sunny conditions of weeks at sea.

F The human population on the Galapagos Islands is limited to 3% (100 square miles/236.5 km²) of the land area of the islands. Approximately 85% of the inhabitants live in the coastal villages. The population has grown rapidly since the 1970s, driven by a rapidly growing tourism industry beginning in the mid 1970s, and heavy government expenditures during Ecuador's oil boom (1972–1983). Migration was fuelled further by a weak economy in mainland Ecuador during the 1980s and 1990s and a boom in sea cucumber fishing (1993–2000). From 1999 to 2005, the population in Galapagos grew by 60%. During much of the 80s and 90s, the population was increasing at more than 6% per year. This rate would double the population in Galapagos every 11 years, but, in part due to immigration controls, the population only doubled over a 20-year period and today is approximately 25,000 inhabitants.

G The year 2007 was an important time in many ways in terms of international, national and local discussions related to the many challenges associated with Galapagos conservation. In April of 2007, the President of Ecuador, Rafael Correa, declared the Galapagos Islands 'at risk' and their protection a national priority. President Correa made this announcement during a visit of a United Nations (UNESCO) delegation which was to determine whether the archipelago should be put on the List of World Heritage Sites in Danger. The decree called for a variety of immediate conservation measures including the restriction of some tourism permits, the return of individuals with 'irregular' residency to the mainland, finding a comprehensive plan to control the spread of invasive species not native to the Galapagos Islands, implementing educational reform, and ensuring the development of sustainable businesses. On June 26, 2007, the World Heritage Committee recommended that the Galapagos Islands be added to UNESCO's List of World Heritage Sites in Danger in hopes of rallying support for their conservation. The Islands were removed from the List of World Heritage Sites in Danger in July 2010 following significant progress made by Ecuador in addressing many of the problems that had been identified. In 2016, the Islands are still off the danger list.

Questions 1–7

The Reading Passage has seven sections, **A–G**.

Choose the correct heading for each section from the list of headings below.

List of Headings	
i Where are the Galapagos Islands?	**1** Section **A**
ii Islands under threat	**2** Section **B**
iii The range of plants and animals	**3** Section **C**
iv The extinction of some animals	**4** Section **D**
v The human impact	**5** Section **E**
vi How are the islands formed?	**6** Section **F**
vii How animals arrived on the islands	**7** Section **G**
viii What makes the islands so unique?	

Questions 8–14

Do the following statements agree with the claims of the writer in the Reading Passage?

Write:

> **YES** if the statement agrees with the claims of the writer
> **NO** if the statement contradicts the claims of the writer
> **NOT GIVEN** if it is impossible to say what the writer thinks about this

8 The islands are all very different ages.

9 The animals and plants are quite unique.

10 The islands are owned by Ecuador.

11 The plants and animals did not have to travel far to get to the islands.

12 All animals swam to the islands.

13 The population is likely to continue to grow.

14 The government's plan covered all areas it needed to.

Language focus: Articles

(G) Grammar reference on page 225 of the Student's Book.

1 Complete the rules for articles **1–8** using *a/an, the* or the zero article. Then match the rules to the sentences **a–i** below. Some rules match to more than one sentence.

1 We use _____ only with a singular noun.

2 _____ goes with single, plural and uncountable nouns.

3 We use _____ when we have already mentioned something.

4 We use _____ when there is only one thing.

5 We use _____ when the speaker/listener knows which one we are talking about.

6 We use _____ when we don't know which one the speaker is referring to.

7 We use _____ when we use a plural noun or an uncountable noun that has a meaning on its own.

8 We use _____ when we talk about some places or institutions.

a Sally starts college on Monday.

b I work in a school in London.

c I like relaxing by the sea.

d We stayed in a holiday cottage. The holiday cottage was really cosy.

e He gave the taxi driver a note.

f It's the biggest hotel in town.

g The government are not very popular at the moment.

h Holidays in Spain are very popular with British and German tourists.

i I like going out for a walk in the morning.

2 Correct the use of articles in the conversation.

A: What are you doing this weekend?

B: We're having the short break in Paris.

A: Wonderful! I love a city. It's so romantic. Where are you staying?

B: We're staying in the small hotel in Montmarte. A hotel was a recommendation from Jason's parents. You studied there, didn't you?

A: I did. I went to the university there in 2015. I had the flat on the edge of the city though, not in a tourist area. It's too expensive. Have you decided what to do?

B: I want to see all of a famous sights – the Eiffel Tower, the Louvre, have the lunch in Le Marais, but Jason wants to do other things.

A: What does he want to do?

B: He wants to walk around Petite Ceinture. It's an old abandoned railway line around centre of Paris. He wants to go to a restaurant called Dans le Noir. You eat the dinner in the dark! And he wants to go to a French naval history museum!

A: Oh, quite different then. How are you getting there?

B: We're taking train from London.

Writing
Task 2

1 Read the Task 2 question below. Then answer questions **1** and **2** which follow.

WRITING TASK 2

You should spend about 40 minutes on this task.

Write about the following topic:

> *Some people think that international travel is damaging to local cultures.*
> *Others, however, say that it has a positive effect on culture.*
> *Discuss both these views and give your own opinion.*

Give reasons for your answer and include any relevant examples from your own knowledge or experience.

Write at least 250 words.

---

    1 Complete the paraphrase of the question:

       Do I think _____ is good or _____ for local cultures?

    2 In addition to the two sides of the argument, what else do you need to give?

2 Skim the model answer on page 99 and decide which is the correct outline below, **A** or **B**.

Outline A

1 introduction with opinion

2 positive effect of international travel on local cultures

3 disadvantages of international travel on local cultures

4 conclusion

Outline B

1 introduction with opinion

2 advantages and disadvantages of international travel on local cultures

3 positive effect of local travel

4 conclusion

3 Decide which of the ideas, **1–8**, below you think are most relevant to the Task 2 question. If it is irrelevant mark it with an **X**. Then add your own ideas to the list.

    1 local food is changing and styles of cooking are being lost ☐

    2 traditional forms of entertainment are disappearing ☐

    3 governments are working more closely ☐

    4 global brands and products are pushing out local ones ☐

    5 wider positive exposure to other cultures ☐

    6 it's increasing climate change ☐

    7 better infrastructure ☐

    8 increased cultural understanding ☐

4 Generate ideas for your essay by thinking of the opposites of the relevant ideas in exercise 3. Can you think of examples to support your ideas?

5 Read the introduction in the model answer below and identify the missing articles.

6 Insert sentences **a**, **b** and **c** into the model answer and explain their purpose.

    a Whether that is the global brand of a sport such as premier league football, or one of a film or music star, it still arguably removes an opportunity for local brands, musicians and actors.

    b For instance, better infrastructures have been built due to the increased income from tourism.

    c While there has been a benefit to many cultures as a result, there can be no denying that much has been lost because of this.

> In the last century, the increase in international travel has meant world has become much smaller place and, arguably, the cultures within it have become more and more similar. **1** _____
>
> Globalisation and international travel have, to a certain extent, enhanced many cultures. International travel has enabled many cultures to improve much about their local society. **2** _____ Furthermore, these local cultures have been able to import various things from around the world. Whether that is food, cinema, music or fashion, it is arguable that this has benefited these cultures as they now have a wider exposure to different tastes, styles and genres.
>
> However, while many view this as a positive, it does, arguably, take something away from the local culture. Local foods are increasingly influenced by international brands, and products such as pizza and burgers are now prevalent throughout the world. In addition, in many societies young people pay more attention to global brands and diminished attention to local ones. **3** _____
>
> In conclusion, while international travel has benefited local communities to some extent, there can be no doubt that it has had a negative impact on many of the local traditions. Change is natural, but it is perhaps the pace of change that is worrying in many cases.

7 Read the model answer again and answer questions **a** and **b**.

    a <u>Underline</u> three verbs of positive change and three of negative change.

    b Ⓒircle linking words to show:

      i another point

      ii an alternative point.

8 Write your own answer for the Task 2 question.

Vocabulary: Nouns related to systems

Wordlist on page 217 of the Student's Book.

1 Match the words that go together.

1 satellite	**a** filter/purification	**i** infrastructure
2 railway	**b** mobile/fibre optic	**ii** network
3 telephone	**c** tunnels/bridges	**iii** system
4 water	**d** dish/communications	**iv** supply
5 gas/oil	**e** host/access	**v** supply
6 electricity	**f** pylons/cables	**vi** grid
7 the internet	**g** pipelines/fields	**vii** web

2 Form a collocation, using all the words **1–7** in exercise 1 and the words in the box below, to complete each sentence. You will need to put one of the words into the correct form.

browsing	network	appliances	industry
~~tunnel~~	purification	channel	supply

Example:

The longest *railway tunnel* in the world is Gotthard Base in Switzerland. It connects Erstfeld station with Bodio through the Alps mountain range.

1 The _____ has been central to the economic growth of many countries in the Middle East. This sector has enabled investment in infrastructure and education.

2 Siemens, who are now best known for mobile communications, started the world's first _____ in Berlin.

3 Twenty per cent of our time online is spent _____ .

4 China has seen the fastest growth in the purchase of _____ at home in the last 20 years. Sales of fridges, freezers and washing machines have grown particularly quickly.

5 Some countries rely on _____ from the sea because they do not have a fresh supply they can drink.

6 The _____ for Europe largely comes from Russia's vast fields.

7 In 1962, over 100 million people watched the first _____ broadcast by Telstar.

Gotthard Base railway tunnel, Switzerland

3 Cross out the word that doesn't belong in each group.

1 Oil industry	satellite	field	exploration	supply
2 Telephone network	browse	satellite	weather	mobile
3 Satellite system	appliance	receiver	channel	broadcast
4 Internet/web	server	industry	connection	host
5 Water supply	tap	field	treatment	well
6 Gas supply	industry	appliance	viaduct	pipeline
7 Electricity grid	access	national	generator	station
8 Railway infrastructure	line	viaduct	pylon	tunnel

 2.6 **SECTION 3** *Questions 21–30*

Questions 21–23

Choose the correct letter, A, B or C.

21 Mia's presentation is about

A disease prevention in the developing world.

B structuring the health system in poorer countries.

C what the short-term impacts of disease prevention are.

22 Jan is finding the research hard because

A he doesn't understand the theory.

B most of the examples are from the media.

C he doesn't understand the topic in English.

23 Mia wants to

A do her presentation for Jan.

B record her presentation.

C tell Jan about the main points.

Questions 24–30

Complete the notes below.

*Write **NO MORE THAN THREE WORDS AND/OR A NUMBER** for each answer.*

24 In poorer countries there is a lack of ....

25 One solution is to offer more money or .... to encourage people
not to leave.

26 Pharmacies across the country need supplies but the drugs are often in ....

27 People do not like to make payment for something prior to it being ....

28 Use .... to check supplies.

29 The current system can mean there is not enough of a drug in ....

30 Using messaging systems .... the number of times regional medical officers
didn't have a drug available.

Word building: Modal verbs to adjectives

1   Complete the table using the words in the box.

likely   expected   certain   unlikely   obligatory   able
essential   necessary   ~~possible~~   ~~probable~~   ~~compulsory~~

Possibility	Probability	Obligation
possible	*probable*	*compulsory*

2   For **1–8** below, decide which sentences are correct. Rewrite the sentences that are incorrect using the correct modal verbs.

1   They don't have to build a new high-speed rail network; it's not certain.

2   The tunnel should be finished in January, but that's only probable and not for certain.

3   Could the internet speed be improved? Yes, it's expected.

4   The company didn't need to spend so much money. It was unnecessary.

5   The government do not want to upgrade the rail network. They are very willing.

6   The internet provided many people with the opportunity to set up their own business. People were possible to put into action a whole range of new ideas.

7   Internet security needs to improve. It's essential because it's becoming more and more vulnerable.

8   It's expected that investment would improve the country's infrastructure dramatically as there is little there in terms of a secure banking system at the moment.

Reading
Questions 1–13

READING PASSAGE

*You should spend about 20 minutes on **Questions 1–13** which are based on the Reading Passage below.*

The rise of the mega-city

by Allister Heath from The Telegraph

In 1800, just 5% of the world's population lived in cities; the rest resided in small towns and villages. In 2014, 54% of the world's population lived in cities. The transformation has been dramatic; urbanisation and the rise of cities is one of the most important changes that humanity has undergone as it has become richer. The trend is set to continue, posing huge challenges in some areas but creating vast opportunities for those willing and able to seize them. It is not just that we are now much more likely to live in cities – more and more of us live in extremely large urban areas. At the start of the 19th century, just one city had a population that was greater than 1 million – Beijing. Now, there are about 500 cities with a population of over 1 million, accounting for 22.7% of the world's total population.

The rise of the mega-city, a city with a population over ten million, is even more striking: 40 years ago, just Tokyo and New York fell into that category, joined by Mexico City in 1975. Today, 35 mega-cities boast 10m or more people. The largest, at 37.6m, is Tokyo, followed by Jakarta (30m), Delhi (24.1m), Seoul (23m) and Manila (22.7m). Some of the mega-cities are shockingly little-known in the West, at least among the general public, including Guangzhou-Foshan, two cities in China's Pearl Delta that are gradually combining into one area, (which counts 18.3m inhabitants) or Nagoya in Japan (10.2m). There will be another 10 or so mega-cities in a decade's time, with an extra six or so in two decades' time, according to forecasts.

All of these facts, and many more, are drawn from *The Problem with Mega-Cities* by Joel Kotkin and colleagues, and published by Chapman University's Centre for Demographics and Policy. While I tend to disagree with many of the book's conclusions, and am more upbeat about cities than its authors are, it is chock-a-block with fascinating insights and statistics.

London was the smallest of the 29 mega-cities, with its urban region (which includes not just Greater London but a swathe of the home counties' commuter belt) now home to 10.15m, compared with 10.98m for the Paris region. Crucially, however, London's population grew at a much faster rate than any other mega-city in the developed world – more than 10% over the past decade, against 8% for Paris, 6% for Los Angeles and just 3% for New York. Net migration figures suggest that London is continuing to expand at a very fast rate, a development which is bound to continue to put pressure on house prices at a time of still limited supply.

Britain's capital city, which has regained much of its erstwhile commercial and cultural greatness, is a good example of how a mega-city drives growth, progress, jobs and prosperity in a wider national economy. But that is not true of every mega-city. According to global management consultants, McKinsey, middle-sized cities rather than mega-cities typically drive global growth.

In the US, New York, despite its recent renaissance, has nevertheless been in continuing relative decline, with corporate headquarters and the centre of economic gravity shifting to places such as Texas. Being a mega-city is not enough: you also need the right economic policies. One of the greatest problems in London, but also in New York, San Francisco and elsewhere, has been over-regulated property markets that have pushed up prices. Many cities fail to get the infrastructure right, creating immense transport problems. Crime and educational failure can be rife. Mega-cities in the emerging world, where almost all of the population growth and urbanisation is being concentrated, suffer especially badly from such intractable issues.

On balance, however, the likes of Harvard's Economics professor, Ed Glaeser, are right: cities are where the action lies, even though many people find the countryside a more pleasant place in which to reside. They facilitate the intensification of the division of labour and knowledge, the specialisation and the trade that fuel progress. The increasing returns to scale from urbanisation may partly be eroded by technology but the general principle will remain. Expect the rise of the mega-city to continue in the years and decades ahead.

Questions 1–9

Complete the summary below.

*Choose **NO MORE THAN TWO WORDS AND/OR A NUMBER** from the passage for each answer.*

Reasons for the rise of the mega-city

The rise of living in cities is linked to how society has **1** .... More of us live in cities and these are becoming very big **2** .... Two centuries ago, only **3** .... had over a million inhabitants.

The largest city in the world today is **4** .... In twenty years' time there will be another sixteen **5** ....

London's population from the **6** .... is over 10 million. The number of inhabitants there grew **7** .... than any other mega-city in the developed world. A mega-city like London can make the **8** .... stronger, however in general, large cities have not caused **9** .... in recent times.

Questions 10–13

Answer the questions below.

*Choose **NO MORE THAN THREE WORDS** from the passage for each answer.*

10 What are there too many rules about in many mega-cities?

11 What issue is caused by poor infrastructure?

12 Where do people prefer to live?

13 What will continue to grow in the coming years?

Language focus: Concession and developing ideas

G Grammar reference on page 226 of the Student's Book.

1 Complete sentences **1–8** with words from the box. More than one option might be possible.

though	although … may	may … but	while … may
nevertheless	much as	but	nonetheless

1 _____ the roads in the area need improving, the government are unlikely to spend the money.

2 The mobile telephone network _____ be improving, _____ it is not a priority.

3 _____ a high-speed rail link is a good idea, the cost _____ be prohibitive.

4 _____ education standards are generally high, they _____ not be of an international standard.

5 The average standard of living has improved dramatically. _____ at least 20% of the population live in poverty.

6 _____ the energy supply has improved, parts of the country still do not have a reliable supply.

7 The development was a success _____ it did not have the infrastructure legacy the government had hoped for.

8 Renewable energy can be expensive to develop. _____ , it is an important part of the country's future energy supply.

2 Match these extreme ideas **a–h** to the sentences in exercise 1.

a We should invest in more primary teachers rather than secondary teachers.

b Income needs to be redistributed.

c Fossil fuels won't run out in my lifetime.

d They tend to waste money on other areas such as military spending.

e Without investing in communications, many areas will fail to attract business investment.

f Billions of dollars is too much money to spend to simply reduce commuting times by a few minutes.

g The country should focus on providing essentials such as this; otherwise it will severely limit people's lives.

h The money could have been better spent elsewhere.

3 The linking words in some of these sentences have been used incorrectly. Correct any that are wrong.

1 Although the road network has been significantly improved, the changes may not be enough to reduce the congestion levels noticeably.

2 The train network may be old. Although it is a vital part of the transport network.

3 The water supply may be reliable but it is not considered clean enough to drink.

4 Nevertheless good communication networks are an important part of society, the costs outweigh the benefits involved in the investment.

5 Many diseases are preventable although people lack access to clean water.

6 Though the government planned the development in a sustainable way there have still been many environmental problems.

1 Read the Task 1 question and answer questions **1–4** below.

WRITING TASK 1

You should spend about 20 minutes on this task.

> The pie charts show the source of electricity in 2000 and 2014 in the UK.
> Summarise the information by selecting and reporting the main features,
> and make comparisons where relevant.

Write at least 150 words.

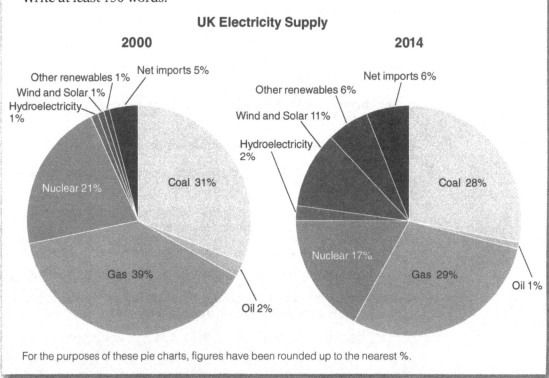

UK Electricity Supply

For the purposes of these pie charts, figures have been rounded up to the nearest %.

1 <u>Underline</u> the correct words in *italics* to describe the main difference between a task with one pie chart and a task with two pie charts.

One/Two pie chart is usually just a *trend/comparison* task.

One/Two pie charts usually indicate *comparison/compare* and a *comparisons/trend*.

2 Use the words in the box to complete the gaps to group the fuels shown in the pie charts.

| renewable   non-renewable   fossil |

a Coal, gas and oil are known as _____ fuels.

b Coal, gas, oil and nuclear energy are _____ fuels.

c Hydroelectricity, wind and solar power are all _____ energy.

3 Look at the pie charts. Which category has seen the biggest fall?

4 Which categories have seen the biggest rise?

2 Complete sentences **a–e** with words from the box.
Which is the introductory sentence for the model answer in exercise 3?

falling by	fuel	respectively	rose from … to
fell from … to	production	reduction	

a Total non-renewable energy use for electricity _____ 93% _____ 75%.

b Renewable energy use _____ 3% _____ just under 20%.

c The data in the pie charts show the source of _____ for electricity _____ in the UK between 2000 and 2014.

d Use of coal and nuclear energy to produce electricity fell by 2% and 4% _____ .

e The main _____ was in the use of gas with levels _____ 10%.

3 Put the remaining sentences from exercise 2 into the correct place in the model answer below.

> **1** _____ . The biggest change overall is the lower dependence on non-renewable energy and the increased use of renewable energy.
> **2** _____ . The use of some fossil fuels has actually changed very little.
> **3** _____ . **4** _____ . This fall has been made up for by the increasing use of renewable energy. **5** _____ . Hydroelectricity has shown very little growth whereas wind and other renewable sources have increased by a total of 15 per cent. Finally, the UK is importing slightly more of its electricity than it did in 2000.

4 How has the model answer grouped different information from the pie charts?

5 Write your own answer for the Task 1 question.

14 Money and well-being

Vocabulary: Money matters

Wordlist on page 217 of the Student's Book.

1 Match the words **1–8** to the definitions **a–h**.

1	money management	**a**	a place where money can be safely stored
2	money market	**b**	money usually given to children to spend either monthly or weekly
3	pocket money	**c**	a place to trade money
4	money laundering	**d**	looking after and organising your money
5	paper money	**e**	money that has been illegally copied
6	sponsorship money	**f**	money given to someone for doing an activity, e.g. running a race, to raise money, usually for a charity
7	counterfeit money	**g**	to move illegal money to make it appear legal
8	money box	**h**	money in note form, not coins

2 Complete each sentence **1–8** with one of the words from the box. Decide the correct position for the word in the sentence.

finances	cash	currency	limit	~~finance~~
account	consumer	income	debt	

Example:

Local authorities are required to distinguish between revenue and _____ capital __*finance*__ in their accounting.

1 The country's _____ burden _____ has become increasingly high since the financial crisis. The amount it owes is increasing by billions each day.

2 The company is thinking of spending some of the surplus on new premises because its _____ reserves _____ are high.

3 I have reached the _____ credit _____ on my credit card. I can't spend any more money.

4 My wife keeps control of the _____ family _____ . I don't really know what money we have coming in or going out.

5 There have been high levels of _____ fluctuation _____ since the government's decision. The pound fell by 10% but has now recovered about 5%.

6 He has a _____ savings _____ but the interest rate is so low he doesn't put much money in there.

7 _____ spending _____ is at an all-time low. Purchases of luxury goods have especially fallen.

8 I have a lot of shares and I generally live on my _____ investment _____ .

3 Cross out the word that does not collocate with each word **1–9** on the left.

1 finances	**a** government	**b** state	**c** crop
2 savings	**a** bank	**b** plan	**c** transfer
3 currency	**a** consumer	**b** market	**c** speculation
4 credit	**a** terms	**b** bank	**c** transfer
5 debt	**a** mountain	**b** collection	**c** capital
6 income	**a** capital	**b** household	**c** arrangement
7 expenditure	**a** welfare	**b** consumer	**c** public
8 spending	**a** flow	**b** public	**c** government
9 cash	**a** crisis	**b** settlement	**c** speculation

Listening
Section 4

 2.7 SECTION 4 *Questions 31–40*

Questions 31–34

What comments does the lecturer make about these topics?

Choose **FOUR** *answers from the box and write the correct letter,* **A–F**, *next to Questions 31–34.*

Factors which affect our happiness

Topics

31 Crime ....

32 Trust ....

33 Advances in technology ....

34 Television ....

Comments
A increasing levels
B fallen
C stayed the same
D more violent
E changing social life
F more pressure on family

Questions 35–40

Complete the notes below.

Write **NO MORE THAN THREE WORDS AND/OR A NUMBER** *for each answer.*

The effect of TV on our well-being

Television has arguably affected society in many ways.

Television has **35** .... we have for our own life.

People's experiences not limited to their **36** ....

In 1982, half the characters on prime-time TV were **37** ....

How rich we feel depends on **38** .... with others.

For every hour Americans spend watching TV, they spend an extra
39 .... to be the same as other people.

The pressure from advertising is the worst for **40** ....

Word building: Values and beliefs

1 Choose the correct word in *italics* to complete each sentence.

   1 It's the *custom/belief* to give a business card with two hands in Japan.

   2 The company didn't behave *ethically/idealistically* by employing child labour.

   3 By what *standard/moral* are you measuring this?

   4 An important *value/custom* is showing your elders respect.

   5 One of the *standards/beliefs* of our company is to provide everyone with equal opportunities.

   6 Young children learn the *principals/standards* of right and wrong from the adults around them.

   7 The *moral/value* of the story is to not rush things.

   8 He hasn't started working yet and I feel he has an *ideal/idealistic* view of the working world.

2 Complete the sentences with the correct form of the word in brackets.

   1 It is important to _____ the marking so that all students are treated fairly. (standard)

   2 I don't think he acted in a very _____ manner. (ethics)

   3 Individual freedom is _____ by many in our society. (values)

   4 It's _____ to give a small present when going to visit someone. (customs)

   5 We _____ in equal rights for men and women. (beliefs)

   6 He's a very _____ person. (principles)

   7 _____ speaking, I think you made the wrong decision. (morals)

Reading
Questions 1–13

READING PASSAGE

*You should spend about 20 minutes on **Questions 1–13** which are based on the Reading Passage below.*

The pursuit of happiness can be a lifelong search for some – but researchers believe they may have found a key factor in feeling a greater overall sense of wellbeing. Individuals who feel a strong sense of belonging to social groups are much happier people, according to research published in 2016 by psychologists. Nottingham Trent University researchers found that the more an individual identified with a particular group, such as family, in their local community or through a hobby, the happier they were with their life.

Contrary to popular belief, happiness can be bought. According to a 2016 study from the University of Cambridge, we can buy happiness, but only if your spending matches your personality type. People who spent more money on purchases which matched their personality were found to be happier, with spending in the right way mattering more than total income or spending. The study found that those with a particular personality spend more on products that match their personality type. The degree to which this occurred was found to be highly predictive of a person's happiness. For instance, someone who scored highly for 'Agreeableness' tended to spend more on charities and pets, and a greater correlation between those two variables would be predictive of increased happiness.

A weekend relaxing, reading a book or playing with the children might seem like the perfect recipe for contentment, but none of those things actually make Britons very happy, scientists have concluded. Instead, we are much more likely to enjoy birdwatching, gardening, the theatre or going for a run, according to a study in 2015 by the University of Sussex and the London School of Economics. They also found the things that are most likely to make us unhappy. Many of these are connected to work and study – travelling and commuting; being in a meeting, seminar or class. Health also has a significant negative impact on our happiness whether that is being sick ourselves or looking after and caring for another adult.

While certain activities seem positively or negatively to affect our mood, there is a big difference between men and women and their happiness later in life. A study in 2016 from the University of Edinburgh has revealed that men who hold a greater number of jobs (and exhibit other indicators of career instability) between the ages of 15 and 27 are less likely to feel content and accomplished in later life. Brett found that the male participants of the '6-Day Sample Study' who achieved or exceeded career goals they set at the age of 18 were found to believe, in older age, that life had more meaning. 'In men,' explains Brett, 'unstable early careers or lack of goal attainment appears to be negatively related to their subsequent outlook on life, and the degree to which life makes sense in old age.' Women were similarly found to attach importance to life achievements, but different ones to those valued by men. Whilst a stable and established career topped the list of factors conducive to male happiness, female participants were found to be most satisfied and contented once they had reached a high level of education or experienced upward social mobility.

Modern developments may also be having a negative impact on our happiness. According to research in 2015, by the Happiness Research Institute in Copenhagen, giving up Facebook for even just seven days boosts happiness and reduces anger and feelings of loneliness. The report suggests that Facebook distorts our perception of reality – we buy in to the oh-so-fabulous commentary on other people's lives to such an extent that we can't help but evaluate our own less than perfect lives as being inadequate. Not only would many of us feel better by not reading these updates, but we could also gain more time back to do the things that make us happy.

Arguably, we can actually be too happy. It's been well documented that grief or 'broken heart syndrome' can take a physical toll on the body. But according to a study from the University Hospital Zurich, over-excitement can cause 'happy heart' syndrome, which mimics the symptoms of a heart attack. Researchers cited joyful events, such as birthday parties, weddings, or the birth of a grandchild as possible causes. In the ground-breaking book *The Happiness Myth*, historian Jennifer Hecht says there are different types of happiness – most notably contentedness and euphoria. Euphoria is for those moments where you're so happy it's the only thing you can feel: think getting into university, getting engaged or being offered your dream job. Great as these euphoric moments are, they're potentially not very good for you. What we should be looking for, in terms of happiness, is being content. Happy – but not too happy.

Questions 1–7

*Look at the following statements (**Questions 1–7**) and the list of people/institutes below.*

*Match each statement with the correct person or institute, **A–G**.*

1 Security and achievement through work affects men more.

2 Job and education related activities make us unhappy.

3 Exposure to too many really interesting things is a major health risk.

4 What we purchase can have a big impact on our happiness.

5 The people around us affect our happiness.

6 Giving up social media can make us happier.

7 We shouldn't try to have only low levels of happiness.

List of people/institutes

A Nottingham Trent University researchers

B University of Cambridge researchers

C Researchers from the University of Sussex and London School of Economics

D University of Edinburgh researcher Brett

E Happiness Research Institute

F Researchers from the University Hospital Zurich

G Historian Jennifer Hecht

Questions 8–12

Complete the sentences below.

*Choose **NO MORE THAN THREE WORDS AND/OR A NUMBER** from the passage for each answer.*

8 What we spend our money on is more important than .... wealth and money spent.

9 Most things that make us feel negative are linked with ....

10 Stopping using social media for only .... makes us feel more positive.

11 Reading about other individual's lifestyles can make us feel ....

12 .... might actually be bad for us as it might lead to a heart attack.

Question 13

*Choose the correct letter, **A, B, C or D**.*

Which of the following is the most suitable title for the Reading Passage?

A Money makes us happy

B Happiness in life

C Work leads to unhappiness

D Social media makes us unhappy

Language focus: Substitution and ellipsis

Ⓖ Grammar reference on page 226 of the Student's Book.

1 Ⓒircle the words in the second sentence or clause that substitute words in the first.

1 Television has an impact on us when we are young and it continues to do so as we get older.

2 Money has an impact on our levels of happiness. It especially affects us at lower levels of income.

3 Redistributing wealth may have a positive impact on society. Doing so may make people feel more equal.

4 I was unemployed for the first three years of my working life. Being so affected my morale significantly.

5 I went back to university in my late thirties. I did so because I had become disillusioned with the profession I was working in.

6 Changing careers later in life is a challenging decision. However, to do so can often make people feel happier in the long run.

2 Match the sentences **1–7** with a suitable continuation **a–g**. Then <u>underline</u> the words or phrases in **a–g** that have been used to substitute words from sentences **1–7**.

1 Our company has a moral code of conduct.

2 State finances should be used to improve the lives of the poorest in society.

3 It is the custom to let the senior person lead in meetings.

4 I have always given ten per cent of my income to charity.

5 Credit arrangements have increased the individual debt burden.

6 Many TV programmes show very glamorous lifestyles that are unattainable.

7 It's important people try to minimise stress and pressure in their life.

a These could be allocated to basic things such as healthcare.

b I will continue to do so while I can afford it.

c This tells employees the expected standards of behaviour.

d These facilities and their impacts have made life stressful for many.

e Doing so is a sign of respect.

f If they do, then feelings of happiness and contentment may increase.

g Such images can make people feel depressed.

3 For sentence **1–5** below, cross out or replace any unnecessary words.

1 People can be unaware of the values in their own society, because these values are often unwritten.

2 My parents gave me a happy childhood, and I'm very thankful to my parents for giving me this happy childhood.

3 Technology can have a negative impact on relationships. To prevent this negative impact on relationships, we should try to limit our use of technology.

4 Some people believe there is a need for change in government spending. This change in government spending is important for the country's economic stability.

5 Although many people have hundreds of friends on social media, very few of these friends are actually close friends.

1 Look at the following Task 1 question and answer questions **1–4** below.

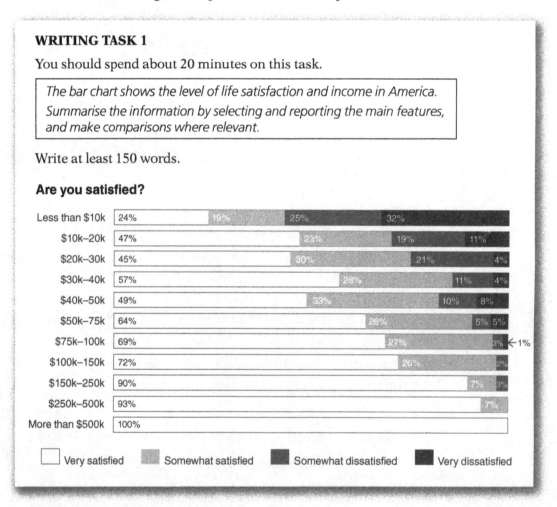

WRITING TASK 1

You should spend about 20 minutes on this task.

The bar chart shows the level of life satisfaction and income in America.
Summarise the information by selecting and reporting the main features,
and make comparisons where relevant.

Write at least 150 words.

Are you satisfied?

Income	Very satisfied	Somewhat satisfied	Somewhat dissatisfied	Very dissatisfied
Less than $10k	24%	19%	25%	32%
$10k–20k	47%	23%	19%	11%
$20k–30k	45%	30%	21%	4%
$30k–40k	57%	28%	11%	4%
$40k–50k	49%	33%	10%	8%
$50k–75k	64%	26%	5%	5%
$75k–100k	69%	27%	3%	←1%
$100k–150k	72%	26%	2%	
$150k–250k	90%	7%	3%	
$250k–500k	93%	7%		
More than $500k	100%			

☐ Very satisfied ▨ Somewhat satisfied ▨ Somewhat dissatisfied ■ Very dissatisfied

1 How many income levels does the bar chart show?

2 How many categories of satisfaction does the bar chart show?

3 Who are the most satisfied?

4 At what level of income does dissatisfaction fall below 10% in total?

2 Complete the gaps **1–5** in the model answer with phrases from the box.

little difference	income group	a link	mirrors	similarity

The bar chart shows changes in well-being in relation to the income earned by individuals in America. The happiest **1**_____ are those who earn over $500,000 a year. There is **2** _____ between low levels of income and dissatisfaction, with more than half of the people earning under $10,000 a year reporting high levels of unhappiness. Increasing your income from 20,000–30,000 to 100,000–150,000 is not always positive. To do so, has little effect on those who are somewhat satisfied. However, in general there is a gradual rise in the number of very satisfied people in relation to income. Having said that, there is a fall from the $30,000–40,000 section and $40,000–50,000. This higher income section almost **3**_____ the $20,000–30,000 category. There is quite a lot of **4** _____ between the income brackets of $75,000–100,000 and the next one. Furthermore, there is **5** _____ in how satisfied the top two are. In conclusion, there is a strong correlation between increasing income and life satisfaction.

3 Read the model answer in exercise 2 again and answer questions **1–5** below.

1 What is the highlighted word 'those' substituting in the sentence it appears in?

2 In the first highlighted sentence, what same word has been left out in the sentence?

3 What does the highlighted phrase 'to do so' substitute in the sentence it appears in?

4 What does the highlighted word 'one' substitute in the sentence it appears in?

5 What words have been left out in the last highlighted sentence?

4 Write your own response to the Writing Task 1 question.

Listening scripts

Unit 1

 1.1

(A = Andrea; R = Representative)

A: Hi. My name's Andrea. I'm calling to find out about the holiday camp you're launching this summer. I'm interested in sending my children there.

R: Sure. What would you like to know?

A: What age groups can come to your camp?

R: We have our junior camp for 5 to 10 year olds and then our senior camp is for 11 to 16 year olds.

A: OK. Can I ask you some questions about the senior camp?

R: Sure.

A: What time does the camp start?

R: Well … it varies. It can start from 7 am, but this costs more. The standard start time is 8.30 am. Both go on until 6 pm.

A: What do you do on the different days?

R: Well, we start the week with sports activities and do these every other day. This can be indoor or outdoor depending on the weather. On the other two mornings, we do arts activities. Sometimes there will be special themes and other activities as well. The first Tuesday we will go shopping in town.

A: And how about the afternoons?

R: It's free choice. The children choose what they want to do. We have pool tables, table tennis, board games, a swimming pool and playgrounds they can use.

A: OK, do you do any other special days out?

R: Yes, every Wednesday children can sign up for a day trip. It costs an extra £20. Sometimes we go to the beach or a local historical site. In the first week we're going to Cambridge.

A: And how do you involve the families of the children?

R: Parents can stay and play anytime. We also encourage families to come on the trips if you have time. Then at the end of every week, we organise a barbeque for everyone in the evening. Is there anything else you'd like to know?

A: Let me think …

A: Do you have many spaces available?

R: Yes, it's quite far in advance at the moment. We still have 8 weeks to go before the holiday camp begins. Really it's best if you reserve a place a month before the start.

A: OK, that sounds fine. How much is it per child?

R: It varies depending on the number of children you're going to send. How many children are you enquiring about?

A: There would be two of them coming.

R: OK, the basic cost for each one is £325 per week. So that's £650 in total. However, there will be a reduction for the second child.

A: How much?

R: It's a £65 discount.

A: That's good. So, around a fifth off.

R: Exactly, it's a 20% reduction.

A: OK, let me talk to my husband about it and we'll get back to you

R: Sure. Could I take a phone number to get back to you on?

A: It's 07886695719.

R: Thank you. Let me just give you this number. It will give you an extra 5% off the total booking when you use it. It's 0885693190. Just quote the number when you contact us.

A: That's great. Thank you.

Unit 2

 1.2

Welcome. My name's Lynn Harris, and I'm the Director of the science museum. Today, we unveil our exhibition of the House of tomorrow. This follows on from our widely popular Homes of the past exhibition from the spring show. It is being launched in conjunction with our wider exhibition, Cities of the future – or smart cities as they have become known. As many of you will have read in the news, a smart city is one which makes greater use of technology to improve how the town works. In the same way, the aim of modern houses is to use technology to improve how our homes work. We're fortunate with this project to have sponsorship from some of the largest technology companies in the world. Not only are firms investing their money, but they have also researched into and developed the technology that might be used in future homes.

One of the main features of smart homes is their increased energy efficiency. This type of home uses 75% less energy than most modern homes. It also uses three times less water than your typical home. The home will actually produce more energy than it uses for half of the year, meaning it actually uses zero energy. Our featured home uses many similar building techniques to the smart home in California that was built by Honda. California is a particularly hot and dry climate, but the design of the buildings means that they are able to keep the inside 30 degrees Fahrenheit cooler than the outside without the need for air conditioning. The state of California also aims to reduce its water waste by a quarter, and homes like these could go a long way to helping achieve this target.

Before we open the house for you to look at let me just talk briefly about some of the main features. Firstly, traditional bricks are no longer used. The house is built from materials that naturally use less energy to produce. To keep the heat in we have used a number of natural materials such as straw panels. The roof is made of solar panels to generate energy. The house is also designed to make the most of its local environment whether that's in a mountainous region or a desert. Outside the house, the drive is made from recycled plastics and has a charging station for electric self-drive cars. The windows also include a new smart system to change colour depending on the brightness. All of which is obviously operated by Wi-Fi.

So what about inside the house? Well, you'll find innovations everywhere. Let's start in the kitchen. Recipes are projected digitally onto the work surface so you no longer need lots of space for books that become covered in food. All food is registered on the computer system and recipes using these ingredients are suggested every day. People have always found the timing of cooking meals difficult. Dishes often do not cook well because the times are not accurate. The oven will recognise the dish that you have put in and know exactly how to cook it and for how long.

The bathroom has also been significantly transformed. Bathroom scales no longer just provide people's weight. A heavy person is not necessarily fat. It can be due to muscle weight. Now the scales measure your weight, body fat, heart rate and BMI. Not only that, they will also connect to your smartphone and recommend activities and food to improve your health.

Not everyone thinks about the impact technology has on sleep. Scientists have increasingly linked excessive screen use with poor quality sleep and health in recent years. However, technology can actually help with sleep. Surround sound speakers generate calming noises such as the sound of waves or the wind blowing through trees. The lighting in the bedroom also tunes into your body clock to help you to fall gradually asleep and to wake up slowly rather than being suddenly woken by an alarm clock and a bright light.

We think you'll be amazed as you walk through the house, and hope you enjoy the exhibition while it is here for the next 6 weeks.

Unit 3

 1.3

(H = Hayley; M = Mark)

H: Hi Mark, how are you? How's the research for your sports psychology project going?

M: It's going well. I've found out some interesting things.

H: So, what exactly did you decide to focus on?

M: Well, I've been looking at the effects of physical activity on stress. To see whether more exercise can lower the levels and in particular does one type of exercise have a bigger effect than another.

H: That sounds interesting. How did you study that?

M: It was mainly a questionnaire given to people before and after they had done exercise. In total forty people took part in the study and I divided them into four groups.

H: How did you divide them into their groups?

M: Each group had ten people in them. The first group did no exercise. I needed this as the group to compare the other groups to. Basically, there should have been no difference between the first time and the second time they completed the questionnaire.

H: I had something similar in my study. The lecturers seem keen on this in any study. What did the second group do?

M: For the second group, I wanted something they could do individually. So, I asked each person to go for a jog two times a week. I didn't ask them to go far.

H: I hate doing things like that. I'd much rather do something with other people.

M: In that case, you would have been better in the third group. I asked this set to take part in team sports. Again, two times

a week. The last group was quite an interesting one. Some people weren't very keen to be in that group.

H: What did they have to do?

M: They had to do an extreme sport twice a week. This doesn't mean I asked them to bungee jump twice a week. Most did mountain biking or climbing. They were quite difficult though so some people felt nervous.

H: So, which activities were the most effective to reduce stress?

M: Well, of course for the first group there was no change in how much pressure or worry they felt. This is obviously what you would expect from this group.

H: Yes, there would be some problem if that happened. But what about the difference between the other groups? Is one type of exercise more effective?

M: In the second group of people it had a reasonable impact. On average this set demonstrated a 20% fall after exercise. This was also fairly consistent across the group.

H: What about the team sports? I think exercising with other people does help but does your study support that?

M: Yes, it does. This group had the biggest reduction in how stressed they felt. It seems that doing activities with others is the best way.

H: And what about the last group?

M: Well, their results were harder to interpret. For some people, it works really well, but not for others. My study showed that their outcome varied the most from person to person. It seems extreme sports aren't for everyone.

Unit 4

 1.4

So what I'm going to look at today is the impact the aviation industry has had on our society and economy. On 17 December, 1903, Orville and Wilbur Wright flew the first airplane just 40 metres in North Carolina.

In 1908 the first ever passenger was Léon Delagrange, who flew from a meadow just outside Paris. The first actual scheduled air service began in Florida on 1 January, 1914. By 2014, over three billion passengers boarded an aircraft annually. Today I'd like to look briefly at the history of the   aviation industry before going into more detail on its social and economic impacts.

Early flights caught people's imagination however commercial aviation was very slow to develop. World War I certainly helped to develop the technology but in the public's mind flying became associated with war and not foreign travel. In 1933 Boeing developed what was considered to be the first modern passenger aircraft. The Boeing 247 accommodated 10 passengers and cruised at 155 miles per hour. Arguably, the plane that changed the world was the DC-3. It was the first aircraft that actually enabled companies to make money from carrying people.

Although planes such as these were significant aviation advances they could fly no higher than 10,000 feet. The reduced levels of oxygen at higher altitudes made people dizzy and ill. The breakthrough came at Boeing when in 1940 it released its first plane with a pressurised cabin. Planes could now fly much higher and faster. The growth in plane building grew dramatically in this period as well. When World War II started in 1939 the US had under 300 transport aircraft. By the end of the war, US aircraft manufacturers were producing 50,000 planes a year!

At this time the first jet engine was also built. Isaac Newton was actually the first person to theorise jet propulsion in the 18th century. However, it was not until the 1930s that the British pilot, Frank Whittle, designed the first jet engine and not until 1943 that the Americans built the first jet plane.

Nineteen sixty-nine marked the debut of another revolutionary aircraft, the Boeing 747. It was the first wide-body plane, with two aisles, an upper deck over the front section and four engines. It was 80% bigger than the largest jet up until that time and could seat 450 passengers. Cheap oil and further improvements in technology have continued to push the growth of the aviation industry.

So how big is the industry and what impact has it had on our society? Well, if the sector were a country, it would be the 19th largest economy in the world! It supports 56.6 million jobs and over two trillion dollars in economic impact. Clearly aviation is indispensable for tourism. Worldwide, 52% of international travel is by plane. However, it is also key to international trade. Air transport helps countries take part in the global economy. The total value of goods moved by air is 35% of all international trade.

On a more local scale, air transport offers a vital lifeline to communities that lack good quality road or rail networks. In many remote communities and small islands, access to essential services such as health care is often only possible by air. Aviation's speed and reliability are also vital when people urgently need assistance during emergencies such as natural disaster, famine and war.

Clearly, though, everything about the sector isn't positive. Airline firms produced 689 million tonnes of carbon dioxide in 2012 and 705 million tonnes in 2013. While this does not sound like the industry is improving, it does when you consider the increased number of flights. CO_2 emissions per kilometre are 70% down since the first jet aircraft in 1943. Airlines currently use traditional derivatives of oil but they are also looking to develop more environmentally friendly fuels. The key one being biofuels – fuels made from plant based products. To date, over 1,500 passenger flights have operated partially on sustainable fuels. By moving to alternative fuels the amount of CO_2 released could be 80% lower per kilometre compared with traditional jet fuel.

Unit 5

 1.5

(R = Representative; C = Customer)

R: Good afternoon. Joyosa developments, how can I help?

C: Hi, I'm calling to find out about your new development in the south of Spain.

R: Sure, what would you like to know?

C: Well, I've read about the development on your website and I see that you have exhibitions showcasing the development throughout the UK. I was wondering when the next one would take place?

R: Sure, booking closes for our next one on the 18th March, the week after next. The actual exhibition itself is on the 23rd March.

C: Where is the exhibition exactly?

R: Do you know the Town Hall in Stafford town centre?

C: I do.

R: Next to the town hall is the Regent Hotel. We will be having the exhibition there. Would you like me to reserve you a ticket?

C: Yes, please. Actually, I'd like to sign up for myself and my partner. Are there any restrictions on numbers?

R: There aren't any restrictions. You can bring up to four children on these tickets as well.

C: That's OK. We only need the two tickets.

R: Would you like me to post the tickets to you?

C: Actually, could you send them by email?

R: Of course. Is there anything else I can help you with today?

C: I can probably find most things out at the exhibition, but could I just check a couple of things as the website isn't completely clear?

R: Sure, no problem.

C: Does the site have its own private beach?

R: There's a beach within 500 metres of the site but it's not actually part of the development.

C: OK. Well, eh, what about a pool? Is there a private pool?

R: The development will have its own pools – a fun pool for children and a leisure pool for adults.

C: Hmmm, what shopping facilities will there be on the site?

R: We'll have a small shop for basic things but for large shops such as your weekly food shop from a supermarket you'll have to go to the main high street. It's just a short walk away, as are the restaurants and bars.

C: Will there be any other leisure facilities?

R: There'll be two children's play areas, a football pitch and tennis court.

C: OK, great. One concern I have is that because it's a new development, what will the transport links be like? We won't have a car in Spain so how will we be able to get around?

R: Although it's a modern development, the location is actually quite central. Outside the front entrance is a tram stop and just around the corner is a bus stop.

C: Ah, how often does the tram come and where does it go to?

R: They are really frequent. The number 12 is the most useful and it comes every 15 minutes. It goes along the coast in the region and stops at every small town along the way.

C: Is it expensive?

R: A single costs two euros fifty. Both ways is four euros. Weekly passes are also available.

C: You mentioned a bus as well. Where does that go from?

R: It leaves from Marco Square every fifteen minutes.

C: And where can you go to?

R: Well, that's the best way if you want to travel to the central areas away from the coast. It's also the best way to get to Water World and it's five euros for a return ticket.

C: Oh yes, the grandchildren have seen that. They're really excited. OK, I think I'll find out other things on the day of the exhibition. See you then.

Unit 6

 1.6

Hello and welcome to Hill Primary School. I've invited you all here this evening to give you more details about an exciting new development for the school. As many of you know, the school has been given permission to use and develop a local woodland into an educational centre for the school. We officially get access to the site from this April, but we have plans to develop the site in time to make use of it from September. Work will then be ongoing until the following January. Initially we will use it for outdoor play for years one and two, but as we develop the facilities, we will open up the access to all school members. In fact, some of the older year groups will help in building the camping area as part of their nature project. In return for being given use of the woodlands the school has been asked to take part in a TV programme highlighting the importance of outdoor play and community developments. All children can take part in this programme, but if you do not want your child to take part there is a form to complete. This was sent with a letter last week and also circulated via email.

So, I'd now like to show you the plans for developing the woodlands. At the bottom here we have the entrance and as you go through, on the left, there's the educational hut. We plan to use this area in our lessons to develop students' scientific and geographical knowledge. We also want to develop the students' practical skills so north of here, on the left, you can see the fire building areas and behind that the den building area. We really want this to be a practical but also fun space.

These small squares you can see in the top left-hand corner are the bird boxes we will be installing. The children will be making these in Art and Design. Then in the long rectangle you can see at the top, below the bird boxes, we will have a bird-watching area for students to observe the behaviour of the birds. On the right-hand side of the woods we have the more 'fun' area. This will be used by our younger students. Next to the hammocks, to the right of the entrance and beside the educational hut, we are having a treehouse built and a rope swing just south of this. There is a playground which is shown by the large rectangle to the right of the den building area. The one education area above the playground is the insect area. Students will have microscopes and other equipment to observe the insects of the woods up close. Below the playground is a large picnic area. When students have lessons before or after lunch they will be able to stay and eat here.

Obviously we have funding to help develop the area but we are always looking for volunteers. If any parents or carers would like to help in July or August by giving time to the development, that would be greatly appreciated. Please sign up at the desk near the door before you leave tonight. The children are already getting involved over the next month when they will compete to design the treehouse. The winning design will be built this summer. OK, well, we have time for a few short questions now but you can always send me questions over the summer via the email address on the screen.

Unit 7

 1.7

(S = Sue; J = Jack)

S: Hi Jack, how's the research for your presentation going?

J: Good. What about your research, Sue?

S: Really well. I've been reading the second edition of a landmark book by Richard Layard called *Happiness: Lessons from a New Science.* It's full of really interesting research.

J: Ah, what have you found out?

S: So the book looks at the main issue of whether we are happier today than we were in the past.

J: What conclusions does it reach?

S: Well essentially, we're not.

J: But we have more money than we had in the past. People are healthier today than they were 50 years ago. My grandparents never took a holiday, I take one every year!

S: Yes, but money has a small impact on our happiness. Many other things affect our happiness more.

J: So if money doesn't make us happy. What does?

S: According to Richard Layard there are a number of factors that affect our happiness, including family relationships, for example, how well we get on with members of our family. The frequency with which we argue has a negative impact on happiness. Another factor is health …

J: Oh I always feel depressed when I'm ill!

S: The main issue is serious pain or mental illness. The way these make us feel has a big impact on us. Two other key factors are personal freedom and personal values. In countries where people have free choice, in other words a democracy, they are generally happier. And personal values, how we feel about ourselves and our philosophy of life affect our happiness.

J: What do you mean by philosophy of life?

S: Well, how we view life. Social groups and community are important to our happiness. Some argue that a sense of belonging can even have an impact on how long we live.

J: So can we say one country is happier than another?

S: To a certain extent, yes. Five main factors: positive family relationships, unemployment rate, level of trust, membership of organisations, and quality of government can all be compared between countries and they account for a large percentage of the difference in happiness.

J: And what do we know about the impact of money?

S: Well, the World Values Survey was started in 1981 and has been carried out six times since; the last time was in 2014. People from nearly 100 countries have answered the survey. It scores people on a scale of happiness from 10 to 100. When someone's income falls by one third their happiness score falls by two points.

J: So quite a small fall really.

S: Exactly! I imagine the thought that you had earned $10,000 dollars less last year seems terrible but for your overall happiness it is not so bad.

J: So what other factors are there?

S: Work is a key factor. Partly the work we do and the satisfaction we get from it, but mainly our job security. For example, had you lost your job last year the negative impact on your happiness would have been high.

J: Interesting, so what's the last factor?

S: The last factor is community and friends. This in particular relates to feeling you can trust people. In countries where trust is high, happiness is generally higher.

J: That sounds like you've got the research right for a really interesting talk.

S: Thanks! I hope so.

Unit 8

 2.1

Today I'd like to look at one of the single biggest migrations in history – the rural to urban migration that has taken place in China. Most countries in Europe have urban populations of over 80% of the citizens, but until recently this number was much lower in China. In recent years it has gone from a predominantly rural country to an increasingly urban one. In research conducted by Kam Wing Chan from the University of Washington, just under half a billion people moved to urban areas between 1979 and 2009. That is the equivalent of the total populations of Mexico and America moving. So what led to this huge migration pattern? It largely comes down to three government policies.

In 1979, China introduced the One Child Policy. This often led to people getting married later and a fall in rural family size to 1.5 children. This fall in rural population led to a drastic drop in the number of agricultural workers. Soon after this, in the mid-1980s, the Hukou (or Huji) System was loosened. This was a residence registration system designed in the 1950s to limit and control internal migration within China. Largely due to this system, the number of internal migrants from the countryside to cities was very limited. China simultaneously introduced its major economic reform – the Reform and Open Policy. Up until this point in time, China had been a relatively closed country, but this policy led to levels of growth never seen before. This growth led to the need for more workers in cities and hence the government reduced the limits of rural to urban migration to allow the growth to continue.

So what has been the impact of this mass urbanisation? According to a report by the China National Bureau of Statistics, 44.4% of new-generation migrant workers work in manufacturing. Those born after 1990 are just seventeen years old when they migrate to the city and, as a result, often have very few years of schooling. On the positive side, this movement of new-generation migrants has significantly reduced levels of poverty in the country by increasing the income for many poorer families.

One of the biggest concerns regarding migration is the impact on people's health. The lack of affordable healthcare for many along with the overpopulation in certain urban areas has led to poor ratios of doctors to patients in certain parts of China. People also now eat increasing amounts of fast food and meat as salaries have increased. What was once too expensive for many is consumed in much greater quantities. As a result, health-related issues, such as obesity, have become a growing concern.

On the plus side, there have also been many positive developments in healthcare in China. Life expectancy is higher in cities than in rural areas. Infant mortality, or child deaths, is also much lower. Children under the age of one have an 86% survival rate in cities compared to 66% in rural areas. Furthermore, only 3% of children in urban areas are malnourished compared with 14% in rural areas.

Lifestyles have also dramatically changed with ownership of cars, televisions, computers and white goods (for example, washing machines, refrigerators, clothes dryers) all increasing in urban areas. The people growing up in cities today tend to have higher literacy rates and urban residents tend to pursue higher levels of education as more and more go to university as opposed to those living in rural areas.

 2.2

(A = student A; B = student B)

A: I'm really enjoying this travel and tourism degree. I think it's going to be very practical for getting a job.

B: Definitely! This project and presentation is exactly the kind of thing you might do if you were managing a tour operator.

A: It is. Right, so we've decided to focus on New York. Are we going to do the traditional sights like The Empire State Building and the Statue of Liberty?

B: No, I think we should plan an alternative tour, to show people a different side of the city; one they couldn't just find in five minutes on Google.

A: Really? But the Empire State Building is so famous.

B: It is, but it's also quite ugly and there are often long queues.

A: How about starting the tour with a breakfast somewhere? Tours always make people go place to place to place. We could plan a whole day out with food, shopping and sights.

B: That's a really good idea. How about starting the day in Louie's Manhasset? They serve great breakfasts there.

A: That sounds good, but I also think we need a specific focus for the day. How about focusing on beautiful places?

B: Yes, that's a great idea. Why don't we start the day at the Nassau County Museum of Art? There is an admission fee for the museum but the gardens are free to visit.

A: What's so special about the gardens and the museum?

B: Well, the landscape of the gardens is very traditional. They have gazebos, flower beds and old trees, but these are mixed with contemporary sculpture.

A: Some people really hate modern art though. Is there any traditional work there?

B: Mmm, less so in the garden. The point is traditional landscapes, nature and modern art. However, in the museum there are over 500 works by famous 19th and 20th century artists, including paintings and drawings.

A: OK, that sounds good. Perhaps we could provide a picnic in the grounds in the spring, summer and autumn?

B: That sounds good. We'd need to find a local catering firm for that. How about the afternoon?

A: We could take people to Long Island Museum. For those that like history there is a lot to learn, but also they have ever-changing displays of American art. Then in the evening, we could go to Little Italy for dinner. The traditional architecture there has been made famous in many movies.

B: Great! So we need to work out the financial aspects of the tour for the business plan in the project. We need to work out how much we will need to spend on each person, how much we need to spend on the tour guide and how many tickets we need to sell to make the tour profitable.

A: OK, well the cost per person is very little. Everything on the tour is free so we simply need coach hire. I think a fifty-seater coach costs about $500 for the day. So a full coach is $10 per person.

B: Yes, but if we only sell half of the tickets the cost will be $20 per person. Is there any way we can make money from other things to cover this risk a bit?

A: Well, we could make deals with restaurants in Little Italy. Lots of restaurants would be very happy to get a coach of 50 people. They could offer a discount to our customers and we could take a percentage for providing them with so many diners. What do you think?

B: Great idea. Let's look at some restaurants and try to work out the possible profit. Budgeting is going to be a key part of the assessment.

 2.3

Thank you all for coming today. I know you're all keen to find out about the college play and to be involved. As always we will need lots of volunteers for various parts of the production and there are many ways you can get involved. So, today I'd like to update you on when we are going to make various decisions. As you will have all seen from the voting on the website, we are down to the three final choices of Shakespeare plays and we expect to know the final chosen play by this Friday. Many of you have already expressed interest in production and acting roles. Obviously, the first person we need to appoint is the director. Once we've done this we will be moving on to put in place the team who will cast the actors and support the director in all elements of the production. We hope to have all of this done as soon as possible, at which point we will start the auditions to select our lead actors. Shortly after, work will also begin on designing and building the sets. Obviously, depending on the play we choose, some of the sets will require a lot more work. At the same time we will be creating the costumes for the actors. We do have the help of two other departments for this, but if you have talents in these areas I can put you in touch with the right people to speak to. We are also looking for volunteers to help promote the play on social media and to start a basic website for us. The website will need to take payments for tickets so whoever helps develop this will need a certain level of skill.

OK, so that gives you an idea of what will be happening and when. Now, looking around the room, I see many faces of people who have spoken to me about acting in the play. In late March we will begin auditions for parts in the play. So keep an eye on your emails for dates. Now, I'd like to introduce a few other people here today. As I'm sure you're aware, putting on such a large production means we will be using people from departments all across the campus and not just the media department. Mary Smith is here representing our Art School and they will be leading in the creation of the scenery. If you'd like to get involved in set design Mary will be available to speak to you at the end of this meeting. Secondly, may I introduce Paul Harvey from the Fashion School. As you can imagine the School will be leading in the costume design. Again they will need more volunteers so please speak to Paul later if you'd like to be involved. All in all this process will take us from early March up until the end of June, which is three weeks before the play is due to start. Rehearsals with the full set, costumes and scripts will then

happen on the stage here for these three weeks. The show will open on Friday 22nd July and continues for two weeks. We've scheduled it so late so that it doesn't interfere with your upcoming examinations too much. Now, obviously we want to attract a sell-out audience every night and to do so we will be advertising heavily online and around campus. Tickets will be on sale for £25 and we will start selling tickets at the end of next week. Once we have covered the costs of production all further money raised will go to a local children's charity that uses dance and drama as a form of therapy. Now if I can take some questions...

Unit 11

 2.4

(R = Representative; C = Customer)

R: Hi, Wellington Country Park, How can I help?

C: Hi, I'm just ringing to find out more about your park and whether it's suitable for young families.

R: Oh, it's ideal. Let me tell you a little bit about the park. As you come in the entrance, you'll see to your right some small children's rides and to your left a children's playground.

C: Are the rides included in the entrance fee?

R: No, I'm afraid not. There's a small charge of $2 per ride.

C: OK. My friend told me something about Dinosaur Land. What is that and do you have to pay extra?

R: That's next to our children's playground and it's included in the price. It has large climbable dinosaur models in the woods. The kids love them.

C: Is it OK to bring your own food?

R: It is. We have a picnic area just north of the lake after Dinosaur Land. It's next to a small ice cream shop. The only place we ask people not to eat is near the animals. At the far end of the park, just east of the lake, we have a small farm. Children can buy

food there to feed the animals.

C: Is it possible to stay overnight?

R: It is. Outside the park there's a small hotel, but in the park we also have a campsite. It's in the south east corner below the children's train station.

C: OK, great. I think we might stay for a night or two. Are there any places to buy food other than the ice cream shop?

R: Yes, next to the campsite we have a small restaurant. If you're camping it opens from 8 am so you can get a cooked breakfast. It's also quieter then as the site doesn't open to the public until later.

C: That sounds good. Are there any other animals apart from the farm?

R: Yes, we have a small zoo, with meerkats, monkeys and birds. This is all along the south of the park.

C: OK great. I think I'd like to book a pitch in the campsite, please.

R: Excellent. Could I just take a few details? Could I take your name?

C: Sure. It's Margaret Dillion. That's m-a-r-g-a-r-e-t and Dillion is with two 'l's and two 'i's.

R: How many nights would you like to book for?

C: Two nights. Friday 24th and Saturday 25th June.

R: When you book for a weekend the Sunday night is free. Would you like to stay the extra night?

C: No, we can't I'm afraid. We have to get back for work.

R: I need to take a deposit of $50. Have you got a card to hand?

C: I do. The long number is 4539 7675 2564 9215.

R: Thank you. And the expiry date?

C: 04/2020.

R: And the security number?

C: 265.

R: Thank you. On the Friday, you can arrive from 8 am. The park doesn't open until 10, but the campsite opens earlier. Could I take a registration number of the vehicle you'll be arriving in?

C: Sure, it's a blue Skoda Octavia, registration EBS247.

R: Thank you. Is there anything else I can help you with?

C: No, I think that's all.

R: We look forward to seeing you in a few weeks.

Unit 12

 2.5

Thank you all for coming today. I hope you're having a relaxing holiday and enjoying your stay in this amazing hotel in Cefalu. Er, I'm just going to take a few minutes now to tell you about the various trips available this week. So, the first trip tomorrow is to the tallest volcano in Europe. The volcano is still active but it's monitored frequently so there should be little danger! We travel there by bus, stopping at one of the local patisseries to sample some local food and drink. Once we have gone as far as we can by bus, we will all take the cable car to the next stage. From there on you can either walk or hire a jeep to the very top. The cost for the whole day trip is 80 euros. This includes the food and cable car but not the jeep for the final stage.

Er, the following day we are offering a trip to the largest archaeological site in the world. Obviously this is a trip for people who enjoy history. You can explore the site on your own or there are guided tours every hour. The Greek temples are in Agrigento on the southern coast, so again we'll be travelling down by coach. This will be from 9 am to 2 pm and costs 30 euros. When we get back in the afternoon, there is a second trip you can go on if you would like. This is to the small inland town of Caltagirone. It means 'castle of jars' in Arabic. The old castles were all destroyed in a large earthquake, but the town is still famous for the ceramics it produces today. These make great souvenirs or gifts to take back after the trip. The trip is from 2 until 5 pm and it costs just 20 euros to cover the coach hire. It doesn't include any food or drinks for the day.

The following day we will go to the famous town of Taormina. The town was the home of the English writer D H Lawrence. It's also well known for its amazing views and historic streets to walk through. Some of the best views come from the ancient Greek theatre we will visit in the morning. From here, to your left, you have amazing views across the bay and on a clear day, to your right, you can see Mount Etna. There's a small, but beautiful beach you can take the cable car down to visit in the afternoon and go for a swim out to the small island of Isola Bella. This trip will be all day Wednesday and costs 50 euros which includes the coach but not the cable car.

On Thursday, we will move back to the north coast and visit the capital city of Palermo. This sprawling city is home to just under 700,000 people and the city is full of ancient buildings which we will visit. There will also be a chance to do some shopping if you would like to. It's also a great opportunity to try some local food in the street markets throughout the town. This is again another full day trip, and the cost of the trip is 65 euros per person.

Finally, the last activity we will be offering is a short trip just down the coast from here to the village of Castel di Tusa. Until a few years ago, this was just a simple fishing village that would never have attracted tourists. Today, it is much more popular since one local resident decided to build an art hotel. Each room in the hotel is designed by a different artist from around the world. There are tours available, but obviously the best thing is to stay there. This trip will take place on Saturday and the cost for a night in an art room is 150 euros. OK, does anyone have any questions about the trips?

Unit 13

 2.6

(M = Mia; J = Jan)

M: Hi Jan, how's your work going?

J: Not too bad. What topic did you decide on for your presentation?

M: Well, I've decided to focus on healthcare infrastructure in the developing world. How's your research?

J: It's OK. There's a lot of information in both the theory and the practical examples but I'm finding it quite hard.

M: Why is that?

J: Well, the examples in the theory books are quite dated. Then the newspapers have lots of examples but they are not from a researcher or a specialist in the area. They're interesting and easy to understand, but the teacher won't let us use journalistic pieces.

M: Sounds hard. I'm a bit worried about delivering my presentation.

J: Why?

M: I've never done a presentation in English.

J: Why don't you record yourself?

M: Oh, I'm not sure I'm ready for that. Can I just talk you through the outline?

J: Sure.

M: So, I thought I'd focus in on three main areas. Firstly, medical professional staffing levels and then pharmaceutical stock levels. Finally, stock management and technology.

J: That sounds like a good way to divide it. So, tell me more about the first issue.

M: Well, in developing countries there is a critical shortage of healthcare workers. For example, in Europe and North America there is roughly one doctor to every 160 to 560 patients. However, in many parts of Africa there is only one doctor to every 20 to 50 thousand people.

J: Wow! That's a huge difference. Obviously more people can be trained but that takes time. Can anything else be done?

M: Well, many trained people leave these poorer countries to go and work in countries where there is more money. Higher salaries or other benefits may persuade people to stay.

J: That's still an expensive solution. Are the other options cheaper?

M: Possibly. The first one – improving communication between donors, governments and emergency pharmacy chains – is really important. Small stores need to be widely available across the country to distribute supplies that tend to sit in large central locations.

J: I guess most countries do not have free healthcare.

M: Often not, and payment is an issue. A payment system needs to be introduced so that patients pay for the medicines when they get them rather than pay when they order them and then have to wait for a delivery. There are issues of trust and shortages of money that mean people do not like to take the risk of paying for something before it is delivered.

J: Mmm, so what's your last point again?

M: Using technology to monitor stock levels. Many places still use a paper system to track stock levels of medical supplies. This can lead to sudden shortages of a medicine in one location.

J: How would technology help?

M: Well, for example, in Tanzania, regional medical officers maintained text contact with central medical supplies. This enabled them to keep better track of the rate each drug was being used at. In three districts, this meant they reduced the drugs they ran out of stock of from 79% to 26%.

J: So they can really monitor use and disease development?

M: Exactly, data is key!

Unit 14

 2.7

So today I'm going to look at what is going wrong in society in terms of factors affecting our happiness. We know largely which things have an impact so why is our society generally not getting happier?

So, to begin with, crime levels have had an effect on people's happiness. While in Britain and America these have fallen in the last few decades, the overall rise in crime is 500% in Britain and 300% in America over the last century. Clearly a rise in crime levels affects people's happiness, but there are other important social changes that have also contributed to low levels of happiness.

Firstly, at different points in time people have been asked the question 'would you say that most people can be trusted?' In Britain and America the number of people who answered yes to this nearly halved in a 40 year period. This trend can help to explain why happiness levels have not really risen.

Domestic and work roles have also changed a lot due to advances in technology. Generally, families have fewer children and the parents live much longer. Domestic chores such as cleaning and washing clothes also became much simpler with changes in technology. This meant that it was much easier for both parents to work. However, this placed increased pressures on the whole family. Couples now had to deal with housework, raising children and having two full-time jobs. In many families there was simply a lack of time to be happy!

With regards to technology, there were no televisions in most homes in the 1950s. Now in Britain over a person's lifetime they will spend more time watching TV than doing paid work. This time has to come from somewhere and it has generally come from social life. People spend less time with others, do fewer sports and are generally less creative. All of which has held back happiness levels.

Television has also impacted on happiness in society in many other ways. It has certainly increased the expectations we have of our personal life. Previously, society was not exposed to such a diverse range of people and experiences. No longer are people's experiences solely confined to their immediate surroundings. They have moved beyond this small group or community to be exposed to a whole range of people through the medium of television. Unfortunately, TV is often quite misrepresentative. For instance, in social dramas on peak time TV in the USA in 1982, fifty per cent of the characters were millionaires. Obviously, there was nowhere near this number in real life. Is this really important? Surely, everyone knows TV is not reality? Well, how rich we feel often does not depend on how much money we have. We feel rich or poor when comparing ourselves with others. If we are constantly being shown more affluent lifestyles, we will feel poorer and less happy. This can actually be seen in changes in purchasing behaviour of people who watch TV. Research has shown that there is a direct link between how much TV we watch and how much we spend. Each hour of television someone watches in the US directly leads to an additional $4 being spent. This behaviour happens because people want to maintain their status in relation to others.

Unfortunately, advertisers tend to target one of the most easily influenced groups of society. It is part of human nature to fit in or copy other people. However, the ones who feel the greatest levels of pressure to keep up with others is young people. Advertisers know this and arguably target this age group more aggressively than any other.

Wordlist

Unit 1

Listening
get back to *phrasal verb*
quote *verb*

Reading
consult *verb*
consulting *noun*
cynically *adverb*
deep *adjective*
draw *verb*
engaged in *adjective*
evaluate *verb*
extrovert *adjective*
form *noun*
grumble *verb*
homeless *adjective*
inhabit *verb*
intimacy *noun*
lead *verb*
maze *noun*
ministry *noun*
mobility *noun*
networking *noun*
notion *noun*
outdated *adjective*
prescriptive *adjective*
psychiatrist *noun*
rate *verb*
robust *adjective*
self-seeking *adjective*
solidarity *noun*
startling *adjective*
strategic *adjective*
toll *noun*
transient *adjective*

Writing
demographic *noun*
hit *verb*
low *noun*
overtake *verb*
peak *noun*
platform *noun*
plummet *verb*
soar *verb*
usage *noun*

Unit 2

Listening
digitally *adverb*
excessive *adjective*
Fahrenheit *noun*
fund *verb*
funding *noun*
measure *verb*
panel *noun*
smartphone *noun*
sponsorship *noun*
unveil *verb*

Reading
apply *verb*
carriage *noun*
coal *noun*
development *noun*
form a partnership *phrase*
hence *adverb*
innovation *noun*
large scale *noun*
machinery *noun*
multiple *adjective*
relate *verb*
repetitive *adjective*
revolutionise *verb*
specialist *adjective*
spin *verb*
trader *noun*
weave *verb*
workshop *noun*

Writing
abuse *noun*
anonymous *adjective*
engage *verb*
enhance *verb*
outweigh *verb*
postal *adjective*
similarly *adverb*

Unit 3

Listening
consistent *adjective*
individually *adverb*
outcome *noun*
pressure *noun*

Reading
Adrenaline rush *noun*
basically *adverb*
bulk *noun*
catastrophic *adjective*
conduct interview *phrase*
creep in *verb*
depiction *noun*
drive *verb*
enthusiast *noun*
extreme sport *noun*
fabric *noun*
focused *adjective*
glimpse *noun*
hedonism *noun*
impulsive *adjective*
impulsivity *noun*
interpret *verb*
led by (to be led by something) *phrasal verb*
meditation *noun*
motivation *noun*
on the contrary *phrase*
participant *noun*
plague *noun*
proportion *noun*
purely *adverb*
reckless *adjective*
sentiment *noun*
span *noun*
specifically *adverb*
thrill *noun*
uninitiated *noun*

Writing
participation *noun*

Unit 4

Listening
accommodate *verb*
aviation *noun*
aviation *adjective*
debut *noun*
emissions *noun*
healthcare *noun*
indispensable *adjective*
partially *adverb*
pressurise *verb*
sector *noun*
sustainable *adjective*

Wordlist

Reading
avenue of opportunity *phrase*
conclude *verb*
fulfil *verb*
leap *noun*
predictable *adjective*
present *verb*
random *adjective*
serendipity *noun*
superstition *noun*
vaccination *noun*

Writing
apprenticeship *noun*
automation *noun*
diversity *noun*
generic *adjective*
phenomenon *noun*
reliant *adjective*
result in *verb*
take to *verb*

Unit 5

Listening
inland *adjective*
restriction *noun*
showcase *verb*

Reading
administration *noun*
bacteria *noun*
cosmetic *adjective*
cut out *verb*
defective *adjective*
discard *verb*
disorder *noun*
DNA *noun*
dub *verb*
elastic *adjective*
elderly (the elderly) *noun*
ethical *adjective*
film *noun*
gene *noun*
genetic *adjective*
genetically modified *adjective*
immune system *noun*
intervention *noun*
lifespan *noun*
mechanism *noun*
modification *noun*
naturally occurring *adjective*
prescribe *verb*

prolong *verb*
replicate *verb*
speculate *verb*
springy *adjective*
suppress *verb*
transplant *noun*
trial *noun*
tweak *verb*
vaccine *noun*
wearable *adjective*
wrinkle *noun*

Writing
anticipate *verb*
expenditure *noun*
housing *noun*
notable *adjective*

Unit 6

Listening
carer *noun*
officially *adverb*
ongoing *adjective*
rectangle *noun*
woodland *noun*

Reading
bamboo *noun*
banquet *noun*
bundle *verb*
cascade *verb*
cherish *verb*
column *noun*
conquer *verb*
continually *adverb*
Equator *noun*
favour *verb*
ferment *verb*
fermentation *noun*
grade *verb*
grind *verb*
heap *noun*
invader *noun*
knead *verb*
legend *noun*
mass *adjective*
mass *noun*
mat *noun*
medicinal *adjective*
mistake for *verb*
native *adjective*
nutritious *adjective*

paste *noun*
pin down *verb*
privilege *noun*
pulverize *verb*
rake *verb*
sack *noun*
sample *verb*
ship *verb*
smoothness *noun*
snap *verb*
stable *adjective*
taste bud *noun*
temper *verb*
thrive *verb*
tragically *adverb*
whereby *adverb*
yield *verb*

Writing
bark *noun*
drum *noun*
plantation *noun*
pulp *noun*
screening *noun*
winnowing *noun*

Unit 7

Listening
account for *phrasal verb*
landmark *adjective*
relate to *phrasal verb*
sue *verb*
to an extent *phrase*

Reading
at the last minute *phrase*
attune *verb*
cartographer *noun*
circadian rhythm *noun*
congress *noun*
deprivation *noun*
ground-breaking *adjective*
immunity *noun*
predispose *verb*
prematurely *adverb*
raft *noun*
shift *noun*
shift *verb*
sync *noun*
tantamount *adjective*

Writing
career *noun*
debatable *adjective*
detrimental *adjective*
distinct *adjective*
drawback *noun*
focus *noun*
focus *verb*
hinder *verb*
hold back *verb*
incorporate *verb*
legacy *noun*
prompt *verb*
scholar *noun*
strength *noun*
undertake *verb*

Unit 8

Listening
affordable *adjective*
come down to *phrasal verb*
drastic *adjective*
equivalent *noun*
infant *noun*
literacy *noun*
loosen *verb*
migration *noun*
mortality *noun*
obesity *noun*
ownership *noun*
predominantly *adverb*
ratio *noun*
residence *noun*
schooling *noun*

Reading
aerial *adjective*
agenda *noun*
allegedly *adverb*
capture *verb*
circumnavigate *verb*
collective *adjective*
comprehensive *noun*
depict *verb*
discrete *adjective*
distortion *noun*
executive *noun*
geometry *noun*
globe *noun*
hiker *noun*
historian *noun*
intersect *verb*

intersecting *adjective*
intrepid *adjective*
landmass *noun*
latitude *noun*
longitude *noun*
manipulate *verb*
Mediterranean *adjective*
millennia *noun*
mobilise *verb*
model *verb*
modernisation *noun*
perfection *noun*
preside *verb*
projection *noun*
pursue *verb*
quest *noun*
renaissance *noun*
resurface *verb*
sketch *verb*
spherical *adjective*
subjective *adjective*
transformation *noun*
undertone *noun*
valorise *verb*

Writing
undergo *verb*

Unit 9

Reading
bland *adjective*
bylaw *noun*
centrepiece *noun*
complement *noun*
component *noun*
corporate *noun*
criteria *noun*
didactic *adjective*
downtown *noun*
establishment *noun*
guideline *noun*
heritage *noun*
indistinguishable *adjective*
individuality *noun*
initiate *verb*
interpretive *adjective*
meticulously *adverb*
patchy *adjective*
preservation *noun*
recreational *adjective*
representation *noun*
revenue *noun*

run down *adjective*
solidify *verb*
standardise *verb*
standards *noun*
swing *verb*
tangible *adjective*
tool *noun*
trigger *verb*
under threat *phrase*
uniqueness *noun*
vibrant *adjective*

Writing
dilapidated *adjective*
envision *verb*
iconic *adjective*
lighten *verb*
oppressed *adjective*
rejuvenate *verb*
scenario *noun*
simplistic *adjective*
skyline *noun*

Unit 10

Listening
appoint *verb*
audition *noun*
cast *verb*
keep an eye on *phrase*
move on *phrasal verb*
raise (money) *verb*
upcoming *adjective*

Reading
anchor *noun*
conceive *verb*
deal *verb*
density *noun*
dock *noun*
enrich *verb*
exhibit *verb*
extensively *adverb*
high-density *adjective*
installation *noun*
labour *noun*
opening *noun*
pier *noun*
preparatory *adjective*
scout *verb*
shimmering *adjective*
sketch *noun*
ultimately *adverb*

Wordlist

undulate *verb*
viewing *noun*

Writing
census *noun*
generational *adjective*
likelihood *noun*
loss *noun*
oversubscribe *verb*
surplus *noun*

Unit 11

Listening
expiry *noun*
representative *adjective*

Reading
accelerate *verb*
arguably *adverb*
characterise *verb*
comeback *noun*
disparity *noun*
enact *verb*
enactment *noun*
formation *noun*
geographic *adjective*
inactivity *noun*
incentive *noun*
interaction *noun*
intergenerational *adjective*
kin *noun*
median *adjective*
mount *verb*
mountainous *adjective*
namely *adverb*
outlive *verb*
prosperous *adjective*
reversal *noun*
spouse *noun*
temperate *adjective*

Writing
amid *preposition*
commute *verb*
distinctive *adjective*
fascinate *verb*
inevitably *adverb*

Unit 12

Listening
archaeological *adjective*

cable car *noun*
ceramics *noun*
guided *adjective*

Reading
abundance *noun*
address *verb*
correlate *verb*
delegation *noun*
determine *verb*
dispersal *noun*
double *verb*
ecosystem *noun*
equatorial *adjective*
fuel *verb*
harsh *adjective*
mammal *noun*
permit *noun*
perpetually *adverb*
reform *noun*
reptile *noun*
tectonic plate *noun*
vegetation *noun*

Writing
bound to *adjective*
diminish *verb*
exposure *noun*
genre *noun*
globalisation *noun*
infrastructure *noun*
prevalent *adjective*

Unit 13

Listening
dated *adjective*
donor *noun*
journalistic *adjective*
outline *noun*

Reading
boast *verb*
commuter belt *noun*
erode *verb*
erstwhile *adjective*
facilitate *verb*
humanity *noun*
identify with *verb*
immense *adjective*
insight *noun*
intensification *noun*
intractable *adjective*
pose *verb*

principle *adjective*
prosperity *noun*
put pressure on *phrase*
regulate *verb*
reside *verb*
specialisation *noun*
urbanisation *noun*

Writing
dependence *noun*
renewable *adjective*

Unit 14

Listening
affluent *adjective*
chore *noun*
halve *verb*
misrepresentative *adjective*
place *verb*
solely *adverb*

Reading
accomplish *verb*
accomplished *adjective*
attainment *noun*
conducive *adjective*
contented *adjective*
distort *verb*
euphoria *noun*
euphoric *adjective*
exceed *verb*
fabulous *adjective*
inadequate *adjective*
indicator *noun*
instability *noun*
joyful *adjective*
lifelong *adjective*
loneliness *noun*
mimic *verb*
notably *adverb*
outlook *noun*
perception *noun*
pursuit *noun*
subsequent *adjective*
syndrome *noun*
unstable *adjective*
update *noun*
variable *noun*
well-being *noun*